A Proverbs Driven Life

A Proverbs Driven Life

Timeless Wisdom for Your Words,
Work, Wealth, and Relationships

ANTHONY SELVAGGIO

Shepherd Press
Wapwallopen, Pennsylvania

A Proverbs Driven Life
©2008 by Anthony Selvaggio

ISBN 978-0-9815400-5-4

Page design and typesetting by Lakeside Design Plus
Cover design by Tobias' Outerwear for Books

Printed in the United States of America

VP   16   15   14   13   12   11   10   09   08
           9   8   7   6   5   4   3   2   1

This book is dedicated to my children, Katherine and James. May you always listen to the wisdom of your Heavenly Father.

Contents

Contents

Acknowledgments

I would like to thank the dear saints at the College Hill Reformed Presbyterian Church in Beaver Falls, PA for the privilege of serving them for five years and for providing me with insights which were invaluable to the completion of this work.

I would also like to thank Kevin Meath for his yeoman efforts in editing my work. Kevin made this book better in every respect.

PART ONE

Foundations

A Proverbs-Driven Life values wise living and wise speech as essential and inseparable.

1

Proverbs

For a Life of Wisdom

The proverbs of Solomon son of David, king of Israel: for attaining wisdom.

Proverbs 1:1

---

*T*his is a book about wisdom, which means it's a book about life.

Far more importantly, this is a book about the wisdom God has given us in the book of Proverbs. By this wisdom, we can learn how to live in light of what is really true about ourselves, one another, and this wonderful yet deeply flawed world. Ultimately, therefore, this is a book about life lived for God in the light of divine truth. It's about life as God intends for us to live it.

A Proverbs-Driven Life centers on one particular place in Scripture, the book of Proverbs, because there we find wisdom in an unusually compact form. From there we can also branch out to other of the Bible's Wisdom Books, like Psalms and

Ecclesiastes, and to many additional places in both the Old and New Testaments. To begin with nuggets of wisdom from Proverbs and then examine how other sections of Scripture address the same topics can help us see truth more clearly and deeply, which is vital to gaining wisdom and thereby living a Proverbs-driven life.

So, what is wisdom? One way to put it is that wisdom is an ability to make good decisions based on knowledge, and then act on those decisions in a way that's effective and makes a difference. Let me illustrate.

In November, 2004, my wife and I, embarking on the adventure of a lifetime, boarded a plane for the People's Republic of China. Having struggled for many years to conceive a child, we had prayerfully decided to pursue international adoption. The process was arduous and the wait excruciating, but one day in October, 2004, our adoption agency finally called. A little girl was waiting for us in China. We had less than a month to go get her.

The days leading up to the flight were something of a blur, but now, on that long passage over the Pacific, we had time both to reflect and to anticipate. Although a little anxious about our upcoming transition into parenthood, my wife and I were convinced we were fully prepared. After all, most couples only have about nine months to ready themselves. Our adoption process had taken a full fourteen months, and we had used the time well. We had read and studied a great deal of material, talked about it together, and discussed parenthood with friends. We had made out our checklists and mapped out our strategies. Yes, we were ready for anything.

The plane finally landed and we made our way to the hotel. And a few days later, on a cold afternoon in an unheated government building in the city of Wuhan, a warm bundle was placed in our arms, a beautiful 14-month-old girl. This was one of the greatest days of our lives. We were finally parents! After a whirlwind trip to the local mall for baby clothes, we found ourselves back at our hotel room with our new daughter. Putting down our parcels and taking off our coats, we sat down to admire her and gaze lovingly at one another, amazed and thankful to God for all he had done for us.

That's when chaos began to take hold. Our new daughter, so cute and charming, started to cry.

At first, we responded fairly well. We had a strategy for crying. Got it right out of a book. So we applied the strategy—some cuddles, some rocking, a pacifier, that sort of thing. No effect. Then we applied it again. (After all, as beginners, we may not have done it quite right the first time.) Again, no effect. None at all.

Variations on the strategy didn't work, either. We were improvising freely now, still without results. The minutes dragged on, slowing to a crawl as our baby's pitiable, heart-wrenching cries filled every corner of the room. Glancing at one another, my wife and I acknowledged the trace of panic we saw in each other's eyes. For here we were in a foreign country, far away from friends and family, with an utterly inconsolable baby girl who was now our sole responsibility. As the minutes stretched into hours, and the awful wailing settled down into recurrent bouts of miserable sobbing, all of our preparation and accumulated knowledge about parenthood began to seem completely worthless. Apparently, raising children was going to require more than knowledge.

We had begun to understand. For what we lacked in those first few days in China was not knowledge. What we lacked was wisdom.

Wisdom is More than Knowledge

Information is about facts, and knowledge is about fitting related facts together. But wisdom is about using knowledge well. What my wife and I suffered from in that hotel room is similar to what now afflicts most of the culture, and even the church. We have vast storehouses of information and knowledge, but very little wisdom.

Never before in human history has there been so much knowledge so widely spread among the population. For anyone with an internet connection, access to additional information is essentially limitless. In the church, Christians have never had greater access to information about the Bible and sound theology. Yet at the same time, in both the church and the world, wisdom is in decline. We take great pride in our accumulated knowledge, and our hard drives are packed with data. But in some of the most important areas of life, such as raising children, maintaining healthy relationships, and handling finances responsibly, a great many of us just don't know what to do.

When it comes to the crucial areas covered by this book—words, work, wealth, and relationships—people make a lot of short-sighted, self-centered decisions. It's true that much of the current so-called knowledge pertaining to these areas is actually very bad advice, but while having the right knowledge is vital, it is not sufficient in itself. Most of the knowledge about babies that my wife and I learned before going to China was perfectly accurate. Later, when we had grown in wisdom, it served us well. But accurate knowledge alone does not translate into better decisions or wiser living.

Another factor that can make the pursuit and practice of wisdom challenging is the sheer pace of daily life. The options available to us in the modern world can be so diverse and so distracting that we forget to pay close attention to the beauty, simplicity, and power of the Word of God and what it teaches us. So much of modern life seems to be about adding—adding possessions, adding relationships, adding efficiency, adding income, adding prestige, adding power, adding health, adding leisure. But at the heart of godly wisdom is an ability not to become distracted from those things that are most important in life, and never to set them aside, even as we adapt to certain legitimate changes in society. For amidst all the noise, the data, the trends, the traffic, the hurry, the turmoil, and the bad advice, the Bible remains our sole reliable source of unchanging, timeless wisdom.

God's wisdom flows through the entire Bible. But as we focus in this book on the unique presentation of wisdom found in Proverbs, we will find three strands of teaching that weave together. We will learn that wisdom is supremely valuable. We will learn that our only real choices in life are between wisdom and folly. And best of all, we will learn wisdom itself.

How to Read Proverbs Rightly

In a complicated world, so many aspects of life can be confusing or challenging that we may grasp at anything that looks like a simple explanation or solution to a problem. The Bible does, of course, bring stunning clarity to many of the most perplexing questions of life. But this does not mean we can read the Bible—or in this case, the book of Proverbs—casually. Proverbs is not a collection of simplistic formulas for guaranteed success. Nor is it intended as a means to back-test and explain difficulties or moral failures. Rather, Proverbs offers us future-oriented wisdom and guidance so we can make wise decisions and live in ways that please and exalt God. It takes both knowledge and, yes, a measure of wisdom to read Proverbs rightly.

So before we get started, we need some insight into how the book of Proverbs communicates truth. That is, we need wisdom about this particular *form* of wisdom, so that we can apply it rightly. Perhaps the most common error when studying a proverb is to read into it more than it is actually saying. Here are four ways to avoid doing that.

Use Basic Logic

As a first step, a proverb should be read according to the plain meaning of the words, limiting our focus to the central point. Sometimes this is simply a matter of logic. For example, when Proverbs 13:11 says, "Dishonest money dwindles away," this does not allow us to conclude that *if* money dwindles away it *must* have been gained dishonestly. That's not what the verse says. Indeed, dishonest gain is far from the only possible cause of dwindling finances, a point that is made several times in Scripture.

Don't Read Any Proverb in Isolation

This leads us to a second lesson in interpreting Proverbs. We must not look at individual proverbs as if they stand apart from the rest of the Bible. Staying with Proverbs 13:11 as our example, let's recall the Bible's teaching that all material riches are temporary and unreliable, not just those gained dishonestly (see Psalm 49:5–9, 16–17). Scripture interprets itself, and no single verse or passage is self-contained. Proverbs 13:11 must therefore mean that dishonest money is merely temporary and unreliable in a more pronounced way than money gained honestly, because God's blessing and protection are to some degree withheld in the case of dishonesty. Also, the Bible speaks of evil people openly enjoying material prosperity as a result of ill-gotten gains, while experience confirms that there have been wealthy criminals throughout history. Therefore, Proverbs 13:11 cannot mean that every dollar earned dishonestly will inevitably slip through a criminal's fingers in short order.

Don't Put God on Your Timetable

Many proverbs speak of certain actions drawing certain responses from God: rewards for obedience and punishment or discipline for disobedience. When it comes to such matters, one specific way we can avoid reading Proverbs in isolation from the rest of Scripture is to recall this glimpse into the mind of God given us by the apostle Peter: "With the Lord a day is like a thousand years, and a thousand years are like a day" (2 Peter 3:8). While God's timing is always perfect, it is never predictable, for he is outside of time, he created time, and he is not in the least bound by our conceptions of time. Thus, punishment or discipline does not always immediately follow sin, and reward does not always immediately follow obedience. All the promises in the Bible are reliable and true, and not one will be left unfulfilled. But some are fulfilled sooner, some later, and some will only be fulfilled in the age to come.

Bruce Waltke helps us understand delayed rewards when he writes, "God develops the character of his saints by calling them to suffer for the sake of righteousness while living in the hope of eternal life."[1] No greater example of this is possible than the life of our Savior. Jesus left the most perfect existence possible and lived for three decades in humiliation, suffering, and perfect obedience, culminating in his death under the crushing horrors of the cross. Only following his resurrection, some forty-three days after Calvary, did he experience his reward: Being exalted to God's right hand and being given the name that is above every name (Philippians 2:5–11).

Make God the Goal of Your Obedience

At all times, we need to keep in mind the ultimate reason we read Scripture: To know and obey God. Following the way of the wise as set forth in the book of Proverbs *will* help you to avoid paths that lead to ruin. It *will* set you on paths that lead to long life and prosperity. Proverbs *does* offer an infallible guarantee that a Proverbs-driven life will result in spiritual and practical blessings. But it is vitally important to remember that the goal of Proverbs is not finding earthly prosperity or even wisdom itself. The goal of Proverbs is to grow ever closer to the God who is Wisdom. Knowing God is the proper definition of the good life, and the highest goal of the Proverbs-driven life.

Jesus and the Book of Proverbs

The book of Proverbs is one of the best known Old Testament books, both inside and outside Christianity, and a classic of literature in its own right. Christians who look to the crucified and risen Christ as the heart of our faith can be so centered on the twenty-seven New Testament books directly involving Jesus that we may come to see Proverbs and other Old Testament books as somewhat removed from the life and legacy of our Savior.

But there are actually very close connections between Jesus and Proverbs. After all, Jesus himself declared that the entire Old Testament was written about him (Luke 24:44). We should come to every book of the Old Testament seeking to uncover the many connections to Christ. Such connections are certainly present in Proverbs. Here are four of them.

Jesus Lived Wisdom

During his time on earth, Jesus personified the Proverbs-driven life. His life here demonstrated continual wisdom. His every act was wise. Just as he was perfect in every other way, Jesus perfectly lived the wisdom of Proverbs.

The Gospels include only one account from our Lord's youth. Luke records that when Jesus was twelve years old, he entered the Temple courts in Jerusalem and discussed theology with the teachers of the law (Luke 2:41–50), some of the most educated men of the day. During this interchange, young Jesus caused everyone to be "amazed at his understanding." Thus, the first time in Scripture that we see Jesus interacting with others, we come away impressed with his wisdom and understanding.

Indeed, Luke brackets this account with the only two descriptions we have of Jesus' growth from infancy into young manhood, and wisdom is central each time. The first instance refers to Jesus after his presentation at the Temple, when he was perhaps two or three years old. Luke tells us that follow-

20

ing this presentation, Jesus "was filled with wisdom" (2:40). And subsequent to Jesus' conversations in the Temple at age twelve, Luke tells us he "grew in wisdom" (2:52)—even *after* he had amazed the teachers of the law.

As the Gospels go on to richly demonstrate, the entirety of Jesus' adult life was marked by his display and use of wisdom. This is perhaps most powerfully seen in his famous parables, which, like the biblical Proverbs, are a particularly concentrated form of wisdom instruction. Jesus was a man who lived wisdom.

Jesus is Wisdom

Jesus not only displayed wisdom. In a sense, Jesus *is* wisdom. This is a second way in which he is closely tied to the pure expressions of wisdom found in Proverbs.

Look at it this way. The words of Proverbs bear wisdom from God. This wisdom is inherent in who God is, for just as God is the perfection of all holiness and all power, he is also the perfection of all wisdom. God is the only source of true wisdom.

So Proverbs is a perfect expression of God's wisdom, in written form, sent as a gift to help us. Jesus is also a perfect expression of God's wisdom, in divine/human form, sent as a gift to help us. Just as Proverbs is more than words on a page, but is the eternal Word of God, Jesus was more than a man. He is the "Word of Life" who "was from the beginning" (1 John 1:1).

Like Proverbs, Jesus embodies and displays the wisdom which is inherent in the being of God, for Jesus is "wisdom from God," (1 Corinthians 1:30) and the one in whom are "hidden all the treasures of wisdom and knowledge" (Colossians 2:3). To see the perfect representation of the wisdom of God in flesh, look to Jesus. "The Son is the radiance of God's glory and the exact representation of his being" (Hebrews 1:3). To see the perfect representation of the wisdom of God in print, you can do no better than Proverbs.

This is not to say that Proverbs is better or more true than other parts of the Bible. Without a doubt, all Scripture is God-breathed wisdom (2 Timothy 3:16). It is simply to point out that the compact, concentrated manner in which God's wisdom is expressed and presented to us in Proverbs is unique. Much like Jesus, Proverbs embodies God's wisdom in a way that nothing else does or can.

Jesus is the Way of Wisdom

Because Jesus is wisdom, God calls us to choose his way rather than the foolish way of the world. Just as the book of Proverbs contrasts the path of wisdom and the path of folly, the New Testament presents us with a similar choice, contrasting "God's secret wisdom" revealed in Jesus Christ with the world's foolishness (1 Corinthians 2:6–8). Old Testament scholars Raymond Dillard and Tremper Longman describe this particular connection between Proverbs and Jesus:

> [A]s Christians read the book of Proverbs in the light of the continued revelation of the New Testament, they are confronted with the same question as the ancient Israelites, but with a different nuance. Will we dine with Wisdom or with Folly? The Wisdom who beckons us is none other than Jesus Christ, while the folly that attempts to seduce is any created thing that we put in place of the Creator (Romans 1:22–23).[2]

The wise man chooses Jesus, and the fool chooses the folly of this world. Jesus is the way of wisdom.

Jesus Supplies Wisdom

Finally, just like the book of Proverbs, Jesus promises to give wisdom to those who hear and receive his words. Jesus promised this to his original disciples as he told them about the resistance they would face in the future, "For I will give you words and wisdom that none of your adversaries will be able to resist or contradict" (Luke 21:15). This promise was initially fulfilled in both Stephen (Acts 6:3, 10) and Paul

(2 Peter 3:15), but it continues to be a gift promised to the entire church throughout the ages (Ephesians 1:17). Because of Jesus' work on our behalf, wisdom is a gift available for the asking, as James declares: "If any of you lacks wisdom, he should ask God, who gives generously to all without finding fault, and it will be given to him" (James 1:5). Jesus is the giver of wisdom and one of the ways Jesus gives his people wisdom is by providing us with the book of Proverbs.

So as we study the book of Proverbs we must always keep in mind that this book, like the rest of Scripture, reveals the glory of the Lord Jesus Christ. Jesus is the perfectly wise man; he is wisdom, the way of wisdom, and the giver of wisdom. Jesus is a unique expression of wisdom; he is the one who is "greater than Solomon" (Matthew 12:42), author of much of the book of Proverbs.

It is this reality, recognizing that Proverbs is a book about Jesus, that serves as the impetus for living a Proverbs-driven life. As we live wisely according to Proverbs, we are living like Christ. We are being conformed into his image and we are reflecting his glory to the world around us. We can live a Proverbs-driven life because Jesus first lived that life for us. As the one who *lived* wisdom, the one who *is* wisdom, the one who is the *way* of wisdom, and the one who *supplies* wisdom, Jesus is present in Proverbs in a most profound way.

The Privilege of a Proverbs-Driven Life

The book of Proverbs offers you an extraordinary opportunity. For those willing to engage with it, it offers a life lived in the good of God's inspired wisdom. Proverbs offers you the privilege of living God's Word in every aspect of daily life. As we will see in this book, Proverbs provides us with wisdom regarding finances, childrearing, marriage, employment, friendship, and speech.

If your speech is godly, and your economic life is biblically balanced and in its place, and your human relationships are sound and healthy according to Scripture, you've just about got everything covered. This book seeks to organize some of the wisdom of Proverbs under those major topical themes. The goal is to help you more readily access the vast wisdom of the book of Proverbs and thereby experience the privilege of living a Proverbs-driven life to the glory of God.

But this will require more than memorizing a few passages. Proverbs is not a reference book to pull off the shelf when you are stumped by life's difficulties. It is not a set of pat answers to cookie-cutter challenges. Instead, it guides and empowers us to discover answers for ourselves by virtue of having gained wisdom through diligent application. In Proverbs, God acts towards us like the teacher who won't give his student the solution to a math problem because he knows that the student learns more by solving it for himself. Biblical scholar Graeme Goldsworthy describes the challenge of Proverbs:

> The individual proverbs are not detailed expressions of the law of Sinai handed down from God, but human reflections on individual experiences in the light of God's truth. Thus, they show us that being human as God intends means learning to think and act in a godly way. It means that, in revelation, God gives the framework for godly thinking but he will not do our thinking for us. We are responsible for the decisions we make as we seek to be wise (to think in a godly way) and to avoid being foolish (to think in a godless way).[3]

The book of Proverbs will not allow you to be a passive learner, merely soaking up information. It requires you to put God's wisdom to work in your life. Bob Beasley notes that someone once described Proverbs, quite appropriately, as "the Ten Commandments in shoe leather,"[4] for in that book we begin to see how wisdom can be walked out in real life.

Are you ready to actively live the wisdom of God's Word? Are you ready to put into practice the power of Proverbs? If so, you have taken the first step toward living a Proverbs-driven life!

2

Thoughtful, Timely and True

The Marks of Wise Words

A word aptly spoken is like apples of gold in settings of silver.

Proverbs 25:11

---

he armies of Israel were brimming with confidence as they rested in their camp at Gilgal. They had just won two great military victories, decisively defeating the powerful cities of Jericho and Ai. Now, as the soldiers recuperated and readied themselves for the next battle, scouts noticed in the far distance a group of moving figures, their outlines shimmering in the heat. Alerting their commanders, the scouts strained to identify the size of the advancing force. Within moments the Israelites were on alert and prepared for the worst.

But soon they relaxed, for clearly this was no band of aggressors. As the group drew closer, some of the scouts laughed at having been alarmed by such a ragtag band of travelers, with their robes in tatters and sandals nearly falling off their feet. To the Israelites, these pilgrims were clearly not enemies, but merely strangers in a strange land, just like them.

The leader of the group asked for Joshua and said to him and the men around him, "We have come from a distant country; make a treaty with us" (Joshua 9:6). With those words, a simple encounter in the wilderness suddenly became deeply significant. The Israelites had been commanded by God to destroy all the people living in the Promised Land. They knew that to speak a vow of peace was a serious and solemn act that could not be reversed.

Were these travelers from the Promised Land or not? They claimed they weren't. They offered their spoiled food and worn-out clothes as evidence of having come a great distance. Israel's words would now be wise or foolish, with consequences to match. This was a time to be very cautious before speaking. It was a time to petition God for wisdom.

Tragically, Israel chose to rely on themselves and trust their own reason. They "did not ask counsel from the LORD. And Joshua made peace with them and made a covenant with them, to let them live, and the leaders of the congregation swore to them" (Joshua 9:14–15). Israel was now bound by these words. They must keep covenant with the travelers, whoever they were.

A few days later, to Israel's shock, they found they had spoken foolishly. Their rash vow had in fact been made to the Gibeonites, residents of the Promised Land who lived just three days journey from Gilgal. Knowing they could not defeat Israel in battle, the Gibeonites had gained an advantage by cunning, and Israel was now in a peace covenant with a people the Lord had commanded them to destroy. Once again, God's people had relied on themselves rather than their Redeemer. The consequences of their foolish words would last for generations.

Apples of Gold, Settings of Silver

In this summarized account of Israel's fateful encounter with the Gibeonites, we are reminded just how easy—and how harmful—it can be to speak foolishly. Unwise words are no rare event, being, unfortunately, very common among Christians. Surely James was correct when he wrote that "we all stumble in many ways. And if anyone does not stumble in what he says, he is a perfect man, able also to bridle his whole body. . . . no human being can tame the tongue" (James 3:2, 8).

If no one can completely avoid foolish words, then in one sense our speech is a lifelong exercise in damage control. Have you ever hurt someone with hasty, careless words? Ever spread a rumor that proved to be untrue? Ever joined in gossip? Ever watched your poor attempt at humor cause an offense? Have you slandered someone out of spite? Or given bad advice that harmed others? Have you spoken the right words, but at the wrong time? We all have, and the goal is to do so less often.

Yet it is also by words that the gospel is preached, and that we can encourage one another with truth and express godly affection. Paul urges us to speak "what is good for edification according to the need of the moment, that it may give grace to those who hear" (Ephesians 4:29). Scripture repeatedly tells us to bless and encourage one another with our words.

Therefore, our speech is much more than damage control. It's also a lifelong effort to pass along to others the grace and love God has given us. Have you ever blessed and encouraged someone with your words? Ever said just the right thing at the right time? Have you given sound advice which helped to spare someone from suffering and harm? Have you stopped the progress of slander by speaking a gentle word of truth? I'm sure all of us have, and the goal is to do so more consistently.

So while we must be cautious about our words, we can also be hopeful. God is eager to be at work through us as we speak. For most of us, each day offers numerous opportunities to speak wisely, in matters both small and great. The Book of Proverbs has much to teach us about making the most of these opportunities by avoiding foolish speech and pursuing words that are wise.

Let's begin with Proverbs 25:11, which packs a great deal of wisdom into a small space: "A word aptly spoken is like apples of gold in settings of silver." In fact, this wisdom from the pen of King Solomon is a perfect example of what it describes—it explains wise speech and demonstrates it at the same time! Let's look at its component parts.

- Such words are like *gold*: They are inherently and universally valuable and attractive.

- Indeed, they are like *apples* of gold: Their value and attractiveness has been enhanced through skillful craftsmanship that has molded them into a pleasing form.

- These words are in a *setting*: They are presented in a way that is perfectly fitted to the circumstances.

- The setting is *silver*: Although attractive in itself, its very attractiveness enhances its primary purpose—to display the unique beauty of that which it holds.

Such words are described as being "aptly spoken." "Apt" is not a term you hear every day. It means "exactly suitable; appropriate." What makes for such suitable and appropriate speech? How does one go through the day crafting words that are like golden apples in silver settings? I believe Proverbs teaches us that such speech—speech that is biblically wise—can be seen as involving three essential components: thoughtfulness, timeliness, and truth.

28

Speak Thoughtful Words

> The heart of the righteous weighs its answers, but the mouth
> of the wicked gushes evil.
>
> Proverbs 15:28

There is no rewind function on our words. We can never truly take back what we say, as much as we might wish to from time to time. How important, therefore, that we learn from the vivid imagery of this proverb. Do you want your speech to be thoughtful and measured, or will you allow it to be more like a gushing, uncontrolled torrent?

Sometimes in everyday conversation we all speak without thinking—without weighing our words. By God's grace, usually the impulsive speech of Christians isn't full of wickedness and evil, but it can certainly be foolish, as the apostle Peter demonstrated on several occasions. For example, after Jesus described the necessity of his death in no uncertain terms, Peter blurted out, "'Never, Lord!' . . . 'This shall never happen to you!'" (Matthew 16:22). When Jesus told his apostles they would be scattered as a result of his death, Peter let loose another gusher: "Even if all fall away, I will not" (Mark 14:29). In each case, Peter was reacting emotionally rather than responding thoughtfully. Like Israel before the Gibeonites, he trusted his own gut assessment of the situation. In each case his assessment was wrong, and therefore his words were foolish and wrong.

Only the fool speaks in haste, without contemplating the potential implications and ramifications of his words. Only the fool has enough misplaced confidence in his or her own wisdom to trust in the value of whatever unedited thoughts may come to mind. Sad to say, we are all fools from time to time, just like Peter. On one occasion, Peter's words even seem to have crossed the line into being wicked and evil (see Matthew 16:23). And although Peter's life is regularly used

29

to illustrate hasty speech, I doubt he was more foolish than you or I. Aren't you thankful that your worst verbal gushings haven't been preserved as a negative example for the ages?

Smart? Or Wise?

Where Peter helps us see the importance of avoiding impulsive speech in general, the story of the Gibeonites illustrates in particular the importance of our words being wise when they represent a decision, vow, or promise. These are words that commit us to some action or position having significant implications. The episode of Israel and the Gibeonites reminds us that being biblically wise is not the same as being smart.

Words that are truly wise are informed not just by the facts of a situation, but by knowledge of God—his character, purpose, will, and ways. They attain to a higher standard than that of worldly reasoning. To all outward appearances, the story told by the Gibeonites made sense. But Israel was judged to have responded unwisely because they failed to see how significant this decision was. Had they been wiser and less self-reliant they would have taken the time to seek God about the matter.

This is where the difference lay: There was simply too much riding on the Gibeonites' request to leave the matter to a quick decision. In a sense, Israel did not have the *right* to make this decision on their own, because it involved gambling with God's purposes. As people who are not our own, bought with a price, and called to live for the increase of God's Kingdom and glory, we gamble in the same way whenever we fail to seek God about significant decisions.

In my experience as a pastor, I frequently witnessed Christians gambling with God's purposes for their lives. This was most evident in the area of romantic relationships. Younger Christians in particular would often assess their prospective spouses much like Israel assessed the Gibeonites. They relied solely on their reason and the external facts as the basis for entering into a vow. They failed to reflect thoughtfully or inquire deeply of God before speaking a vow meant to last a lifetime.

No doubt each of us have at some time suffered needlessly as a result of making an important decision without weighing it before God. Before we speak words that will obligate us in any significant way, we must evaluate our position in light of God's Word. For a believer, speaking thoughtful words means that we give thought to God and his Word before we speak. Otherwise, our thoughtless words can have devastating consequences. In order to live a Proverbs-driven life, you must speak thoughtful words.

Speak Timely Words

> A man finds joy in giving an apt reply—and how good is a timely word!
>
> Proverbs 15:23

In this proverb, the emphasis is on words that are apt by virtue of their timeliness. To be wise, our words must not only be thoughtfully chosen, but well-timed. This is obviously not the timing of a comedian who knows exactly how long to hold a pause before delivering the punch line. This timing involves a natural and spiritual sensitivity to circumstances which God can help us develop.

Timeliness is an area in which we should all be seeking to grow. While *some* words would of course be wrong on *any* occasion, the book of Ecclesiastes reminds us of the corresponding truth that there are *no* words suitable for *every* occasion. That is, some communications, however true and valid, are simply not the right thing at a given time. "For everything there is a season, and a time for every matter under heaven . . . a time to weep, and a time to laugh; a time to mourn, and a time to dance . . . a time to keep silent, and a time to speak" (Ecclesiastes 3:1, 4, 7). When there is laughter, wisdom rejoices as well. When there is weeping or mourning, wisdom resists bright and chipper comments, knowing that sometimes the greatest blessing is found in the simplicity of silent companionship.

Timeliness is especially necessary when delivering words of reproof or correction, which we are all called to do as a service to Christ and one another. A corrective word that is untimely is a corrective word that is unwise, for however true and valuable it may be, it is far more likely to be ignored, misinterpreted, or dismissed.

This matter of correction between believers can, of course, get tricky. Yes, some people are holy and mature enough that they could humbly receive a word of correction from anyone, at any time, under any circumstances, no matter how well or poorly the correction is delivered. But all those people are sinless and in heaven! The rest of us, until we leave these bodies, will remain to some degree proud, self-centered sinners. And when one proud, self-centered sinner speaks a word of correction to another, wisdom is needed.

This book is not intended to discuss correction generally, so I'll just make two brief points about the timeliness of a corrective word. When you believe a word of correction or reproof is in order, here are two things to consider: the virtues of silence, and the perceived right to speak.

Is it Better to Remain Silent?

The book of Proverbs has a strong bias in favor of silence, or at least the very spare use of words by the wise. Consider, for example, Proverbs 17:27–28, "A man of knowledge uses words with restraint, and a man of understanding is even-tempered. Even a fool is thought wise if he keeps silent, and discerning if he holds his tongue." The second part of this proverb uses humor to reinforce the first part: fools who imitate the wise in their silence can often appear wise...at least for a while!

Proverbs 10:19 emphasizes the linkages between silence, holiness, and wisdom. "When words are many, sin is not absent, but he who holds his tongue is wise" (Proverbs 10:19). Clearly, the default position for the wise person is to say no more than necessary. As we have seen from the book of James, this is because the tongue is so prone to evil and difficult to restrain.

Perhaps you actually do have a helpful word of reproof or correction for someone. If so, that is not a matter to be taken lightly. But such words usually involve an area of sin or foolishness that the person you wish to speak to has been involved with for some time, perhaps many years. Is it necessary that you bring the word *right now*? Is this really a good time to speak it? God's wisdom regarding our speech is clear and simple. If we desire to speak with wisdom, then if we speak at all, we must speak with restraint.

Do I Have the Right to Speak?

From God's perspective, we all have the right to address one another regarding sin and holiness. Here, however, I'm referring to that "right" (and using the term loosely) as it is perceived by the person being spoken to. Sometimes words of correction are untimely and ineffective simply because the recipient believes the giver has not earned the right to speak them. This takes discernment by the person who would do the speaking. Here are some factors to consider.

A word of correction is more likely to be received if the recipient is spiritually mature. He or she will know that God wants us to correct one another graciously, and can speak correction through even a donkey when necessary (Numbers 22:28).

A word of correction is more likely to be received if the giver is seen as spiritually mature. This does not necessarily make that person's advice more valid, but it lowers the "bar of acceptance" when the speaker is easier to respect. David could receive a very strong word of correction from Nathan, the faithful and proven prophet of God.

A word of correction is more likely to be received if the giver and receiver have an established relationship of trust.

33

Once we have confessed sin to a fellow Christian in obedience to James 5:16, it gets easier to continue on that path of being open and honest, about our own sin and our observations of one another. The stronger the relationship, the stronger the word that can be given constructively.

A word of correction is more likely to be received if the giver has sought permission to present it. There is something wonderfully disarming about asking someone if you can share an observation. This places you in a position of humility and suggests a desire to serve the other person, not to nail them with a "gotcha!"

A word of correction is more likely to be received if it has been asked for. This is the best open door of all. Few things would do more to promote sanctification among your friends, family, and fellow church members than if people began genuinely to invite the humble observations of others.

Speak Truthful Words

> Truthful lips endure forever, but a lying tongue lasts only a moment.
>
> Proverbs 12:19

In addition to thoughtful and timely words, we are called to speak truthful words. Proverbs 12:19 uncovers the underlying difference between truthful and false speech. Truthful speech, because it is rooted in the very character of God himself, is eternal. Once spoken, it does not change or decrease in value. But lies change and fade quickly. Like all sin, they may appear true or profitable in the short run (thus their popularity), but that fantasy cannot endure for long. Compared to the eternal nature of truth, lies last only a moment. A wise person therefore seeks to speak only that which is true.

When the book of Proverbs was written, two types of untruthful speech were strictly forbidden in Israel. Both focused on the matter of personal reputation. The first was false testimony, which had primary application to legal matters. Civil contracts in that day were made verbally and in public, attested to by witnesses, thus making personal testimonies crucial. Criminal investigations in that pre-scientific age were not focused on material evidence—the clues that are at the heart of modern detective dramas. Instead, guilt or innocence was generally determined by oral testimony. Two witnesses agreeing with one another was considered conclusive. False testimony in court was therefore condemned even by the secular authorities, for it could cost a person his or her freedom . . . or life.

Of course, false testimony is prohibited in the Ten Commandments (Exodus 20:16), and false speech in general is denounced throughout Scripture (e.g., Leviticus 19:11, Jeremiah 9:3–6, Ephesians 4:25, Colossians 3:9). Even for the Christian, lying can come with surprising ease. But lying is always a losing bet. Lies cannot endure.

The second type of untruthful speech forbidden in Israel was slander and gossip. Slander, by definition, is false information about someone else, while the rumors shared as gossip may be true or false. Yet the Bible classifies gossip as untruthful speech, and every bit as bad as slander, because it shares important characteristics of all false testimony. Most importantly, gossip is often based on lies, and is frequently motivated by a desire to harm another person. As Tremper Longman notes:

> Rumors are negative reports about other people based on uncertain evidence. They are spread to injure people, not to help them. Gossip may ultimately turn out to be true, but that does not exonerate those who speak it to others. If true, then the report is being given to inappropriate people at an inappropriate time.[5]

Sound familiar? Gossip fails the timeliness and thoughtfulness tests as well!

As a pastor, I learned that nothing is more destructive to the health of a church than gossip. How sadly true is the testimony of Proverbs 16:28, "A perverse man stirs up dissension, and a gossip separates close friends." Gossip is inherently destructive to community, destroys relationships, and causes divisions; it "separates close friends."

James' comments on the tongue reveal that the destructive power of gossip in the church is nothing new:

> Likewise the tongue is a small part of the body, but it makes great boasts. Consider what a great forest is set on fire by a small spark. The tongue also is a fire, a world of evil among the parts of the body. It corrupts the whole person, sets the whole course of his life on fire, and is itself set on fire by hell.
>
> James 3:5–6

Gossip can destroy not only a reputation, but entire communities. Under some conditions, a single spark of gossip can quickly engulf a church in the flames of rumor and speculation. At other times, like something smoldering under the surface, the damage may occur more slowly, but be every bit as real.

Why Do We Gossip?

If gossip is so destructive, why do we do it? I think there are two reasons. First, gossip is so common in this fallen world that we can easily perceive it as a relatively minor offense in God's eyes. We tend to see these speech sins as less serious than sins of physical action, like murder and adultery. But such a distinction is completely foreign to the Bible. Murder and adultery may be more dramatic than gossip and slander, but in terms of greater and lesser degrees of sinfulness, Scripture draws no lines.

For example, in Romans 1:29–31, the apostle Paul includes gossip and slander in the list of the perversions describing those who have rejected God:

They have become filled with every kind of wickedness, evil, greed and depravity. They are full of envy, murder, strife, deceit and malice. They are *gossips, slanderers,* God-haters, insolent, arrogant and boastful; they invent ways of doing evil; they disobey their parents; they are senseless, faithless, heartless, ruthless (emphasis mine).

In 1 Corinthians 6:9–10, Paul places slander in the company of many deplorable offenses:

Do you not know that the wicked will not inherit the kingdom of God? Do not be deceived: Neither the sexually immoral nor idolaters nor adulterers nor male prostitutes nor homosexual offenders nor thieves nor the greedy nor drunkards *nor slanderers* nor swindlers will inherit the kingdom of God (emphasis mine).

Second, we engage in gossip simply because we like to. Our sinful nature finds it exciting to share a secret or to air other people's dirty laundry. Gossip feeds our pride and gives us a sense of power and superiority—at someone else's expense.

How to Avoid Gossip

Given that gossip is so destructive, and we are so readily inclined to participate in it, how can we put a stop to its pernicious power over us? Proverbs provides us with two helpful pieces of wisdom to help us quash the power of gossip.

Watch What You Say. "Without wood a fire goes out; without gossip a quarrel dies down" (Proverbs 26:20). The first way to avoid the destructive effects of gossip is to watch what you say. Like a fire among dry kindling, gossip has a voracious appetite. But if we refuse to pass on gossip, we effectively stop its advance, for gossip can only destroy if it is continually fueled.

We must refuse to be the next link in the gossip chain, the next bit of fuel that builds the flame higher. To stop the power of gossip, we need to bridle our tongues by watching what we say.

Watch What You Eat. "The words of a gossip are like choice morsels; they go down to a man's inmost parts" (Proverbs 18:8). Imagine the first few bites of an excellent meal at your favorite restaurant. These are choice morsels—so appealing you can't wait to dig in, and so good you just have to eat more. Gossip, as we all know, can be just as tempting. But however delicious it may taste, gossip is worse for you than junk food. Somehow that juicy bit, when you do consume it, goes deep inside you. It may have tasted good going down, but there's no nutrition in it. In fact, you've ingested a spiritual poison that strikes at the very core of your being. To avoid the poisonous power of gossip, you must refuse to consume it.

False testimony, gossip, and slander are not merely foolish. They promote lies—which are hated by the God of all truth—or harm the reputation of people made in the image of God. But truthful words are wise. They bring health, life, and success to ourselves, our families, our churches, and our communities.

The Gift of Words

Why does God care so much about how we use words? Because words are a gift from him. God's gift of language is woven into everything we are, as humans and especially as Christians. Words were present at the beginning, when God created the universe by speaking. He has told mankind of himself and his ways through his Word, the Bible. He has sent his Son, who is himself the Word of God made flesh. And after this world has passed away, we will use words throughout eternity to glorify God and talk with one another.

Our ability to use words, and our reliance on words, are indications that humanity was made in the image of God. It therefore matters very much to God how we use this precious gift. To accurately reveal God's image in us, we must use words according to his command and purpose.

38

That is why this chapter on our words is foundational. Everything else we learn about in this book—the work we do to serve God and man, the way we use God's gifts of prosperity, and the relationships we build with friends and family—will be applied primarily by the use of words. Get your words wrong, and all else begins to come unraveled. Get them right, and the stage is set for growth in all ways that please the Lord and bring you the true and lasting benefits of a Proverbs-driven life. In a sense, the goal is simple:

> Let no unwholesome word proceed from your mouth
> (rather, let it be thoughtful)
> but only such a word as is good for edification
> (let it be true)
> according to the need of the moment
> (let it be timely)
> so that it will give grace to those who hear.
>   Ephesians 4:29, versified and annotated

As you commit to honoring God with your words, he will increasingly give you the grace to live in the good of this verse.

PART TWO

Work

*A Proverbs-Driven Life practices
a faithful work ethic and faithful
ethics at work.*

3

Of Ants and Sluggards

Work as a Divine Calling

He who works his land will have abundant food, but he who chases fantasies lacks judgment.

Proverbs 12:11

I was apparently born with a belief that life ought to be one long vacation. I'm not sure exactly when it began to dawn on me that this was false, but it was probably about the third time my mother called me in from playing because it was time to clean my room or do some chores.

My fantasy received another serious blow when I started school. Just when I had begun to come to terms with the occasional small task around the house, suddenly I was assaulted by a strict daily schedule and bells summoning me to definite places at definite times. Every moment was structured. Even "playtime" had rules! Before too long, home life, even with its handful of chores and responsibilities, started looking really good. Then one awful day I learned about homework. In a

43

moment, the wall between school and home had been breached, my sanctuary overrun. Work was invading everything.

A few years later, when my allowance could no longer support my growing appetite for possessions, I became familiar with work at a whole new level by getting my first real job. Herding shopping carts in a freezing parking lot and stocking endless cans of peas was no thrill, but every week I got paid. And although I was learning some personal discipline, I was also absorbing a false lesson—that work is only about making money. Why else would I grab a bucket and mop to take care of the latest cleanup in Aisle Three? Punch the clock, collect the paycheck. That worked for me.

My college years began to open my eyes to new concepts about work. I particularly liked this idea of a "career." That sounded a lot better than "work." It had a certain prestige attached to it, seemed like it could be a satisfying thing to do, and apparently it also paid well! I decided I would pursue the career of law.

In law school I learned more about discipline and hard work than ever before. It was even OK that *I* was the one paying *them* to let me to do the work, because one day my glamorous and lucrative career would make it all worthwhile. And a few years later, it actually happened. I became an attorney with a prestigious law firm, complete with the suit and tie, nice desk, paid vacation, and good salary. Clearly, I had arrived. I was certain that here in this sophisticated, well-paying career I would experience all the joy that work had to offer.

But it didn't quite turn out that way. I began to sense that something was missing. There was plenty of work and plenty of pay, but little sense of fulfillment, little sense that what I was doing was truly significant. I realized that anything that took up such a huge portion of my life had to offer me more than income. Lawyer jokes aside, the practice of law can certainly be an honorable and fulfilling calling for some, but at that time it was apparently not *my* calling. So I left the practice of law to become a pastor.

During my years as a pastor I continued to learn new things about work. (Yes, it's true that pastors "serve" their congregations, but trust me—that service is hard work.) I learned, for example, that work can become utterly consuming. Even more so than when I was at the law firm, pastoring obliterated for me the distinction between "working" and "not working." It felt like I never really had a vacation, and by almost any definition of the term I became a "workaholic."

Today, I live somewhat in two worlds. Due to a variety of circumstances, particularly a sense that my wife and I were being called to serve our parents, I transitioned back out of full-time pastoral life. Now I give some of my time to practicing law, but thankfully I am also able to serve actively and regularly in the church. The transition has been challenging but it has also taught me, in ways far deeper than I have ever seen before, that the ultimate purpose of work is neither income, nor prestige, nor self-fulfillment. Rather, it is to bring glory to God. That's what it means for work to be a *calling*.

God calls us to a particular role, for a season or for a lifetime. That calling requires us to work. Along with God's call comes the grace to perform that work well, the ultimate purpose being to display his glory. In one sense, I'm amazed it took me thirty-eight years to learn these lessons. But at the same time I'm sure I can still learn them more deeply and thoroughly. Maybe you can too. If you ever resent your work, or find it consuming you, this chapter is for you. And since some of the hardest jobs in the world are unpaid, I'm speaking here to everyone who *works*, not just those who earn money.

Why is There Work?

For most of its existence, the United States has prided itself on its industry and hard work. Historically, the "Protestant work ethic"—work hard and work honestly—has been a pillar of our national character, and a core part of the American ethos.

Where did that work ethic come from? Did it simply spring out of the American character, as men and women eager for freedom and a new start poured into the New World from every corner of the globe? Actually, it began a little earlier than that.

The concept of a work ethic goes all the way back to the book of beginnings—Genesis. We see in Genesis that God is a God who works. He created the world in six days and rested from his work on the seventh day. When God created man he made us in his own image and likeness; that is, we share some of his attributes. One way in which we resemble God is that, like him, we are to engage in work. The biblical work ethic was established when God commanded Adam to subdue the earth (Genesis 1:27–28) and to "work" the garden (Genesis 2:15). The Bible shows us that work is not a curse, nor is it a product of sin, but rather it was given to man as a blessing—even before Adam and Eve sinned. Yes, the curse has made our work harder. There are now thorns and thistles and we work the ground by the sweat of our brow (Genesis 3:18–19). But work itself is not part of the curse, rather it is a calling and blessing from God. Therefore, we should pursue our work with faithfulness and vigor in order to bring glory to the One who gave us this calling. This is the heart of the biblical work ethic.

But that ethic has fallen on rough times in America. As James Patterson and Peter Kim pointed out as far back as 1991:

> [The] Protestant [work] ethic is long gone from today's American workplace. Workers around America frankly admit that they spend more than 20 percent (seven hours a week) of their time at work totally goofing off. That amounts to a four-day work week across the nation.[6]

This, mind you, was *before* the widespread use of the internet. Today, of course, there are countless ways in which workers can use the internet to be very busy yet completely unproductive. There are even websites that make a mockery of employment, with names like Ishouldbeworking.com and Boredatwork.com.[7] A 2003 study found that 23 million American workers are "actively disengaged" from their work.[8] Clearly, as a whole, the US has largely abandoned the biblical view of work.

The work ethic established in Genesis is also a major emphasis in the Book of Proverbs. A Proverbs-driven life is one that works hard for the glory of God. Embodying a biblical work ethic, and seeing work as truly a calling from God, is a core part of our purpose.

Conceiving of Work as a Calling

At the simplest level, *work is any set of tasks to be performed in pursuit of a particular goal.* Notice there is no mention of money in that statement. That's because, as noted earlier, and as I learned growing up, work is not just cash in exchange for labor. In many cases, of course, a worker *does* get paid. But some people (such as artists) work with a *hope* of getting paid, some (such as college and grad students) pay others to let them work, and some (such as at-home moms) do their work for rewards that are not financial at all. Executives, pastors, athletes, parents, service workers, missionaries, students, musicians, bloggers, retirees, entrepreneurs—every one of these perform work: a set of tasks in pursuit of a goal. Almost regardless of one's phase of life, nearly everyone works.

We are all tempted toward two extremes in our attitude towards our work. At one extreme we can be burdened, resentful, whining, shirking, unappreciative, and lazy. When I adopt this view, I become what the Bible calls a sluggard. The sluggard sees work as nothing more than a necessary inconvenience en route to the true goal of life—not working! At the other extreme we can worship our work, finding the very core of our identity in "what we do." When I adopt this view, I become what the Bible calls an idolater—specifically, in today's language, a workaholic.

Left to ourselves, we will quickly gravitate to one extreme or the other—the self-centered sluggard who places work too low on life's ladder of priorities, or the idolatrous workaholic who places it too high, above where God would have it and above our responsibilities to others. But the Bible also offers us God's perspective on work. When examined through the lens of Scripture, work is neither a drudgery nor an idol. As we have seen, God intends work to be a *calling* in which we find personal satisfaction and, more importantly, in which we can glorify the living God in at least two important ways. First, in the productivity and creativity of our work, we echo God's work in creating and sustaining all that exists. And second, as we confront the challenges of our work, our grace-motivated responses demonstrate the fruit of God's Spirit in us.

Seeing work as a calling from God is therefore not merely a balanced, helpful perspective; not just "a good way to look at it." It is reality. God has created us and saved us, and keeps us here on earth to display his glory as we gladly embrace and pursue our individual callings. This gives spiritual significance to our every act of work. How easy it is to demean our work by thinking of it as "unspiritual." Paul Helm accurately describes this mindset:

> Christians have become accustomed to think of themselves as having a "spiritual life" which is sharply distinct from the every-day life in the family, and from work and leisure. A "spiritual life" is a life of prayer and watchfulness, of Bible-reading and church-going. As a result of this distortion, instead of the Christian life being thought of as an integrated whole, it is

artificially broken up into compartments which have little or nothing to do with one another....It is as if Christian responsibility ceases at the church porch, as if the Christian gospel has nothing to do with the pavement outside and the roads and motorways beyond.[9]

The Bible will not allow for this type of dual-mindedness. Instead it beckons us, as Christians, to view our whole lives, including our work, as consecrated to God. The apostle Paul instructs us in 1 Corinthians 10:31, "So whether you eat or drink or whatever you do, do it all for the glory of God." Here Paul issues a clear, universal, unqualified statement. We are to view everything we do, even seemingly mundane things like eating and drinking, as opportunities to glorify God. There's simply no question that work is included in the phrase "whatever you do." Therefore, work is a way in which we can and should glorify God.

Your work and mine, be it paid or unpaid, is spiritual in nature. If work is "any set of tasks performed in pursuit of a goal," then most of us are "workers" longer than we are employees, longer than we pursue a career, longer than we are parents, and longer than we are spouses. Let's see what the Book of Proverbs can teach us about a proper, biblical, and spiritual approach to the Christian's life-long role of worker for the glory of God.

Consider the Ant

Go to the ant, you sluggard; consider its ways and be wise! It has no commander, no overseer or ruler, yet it stores its provisions in summer and gathers its food at harvest. How long will you lie there, you sluggard? When will you get up from your sleep? A little sleep, a little slumber, a little folding of the hands to rest—and poverty will come on you like a bandit and scarcity like an armed man.

Proverbs 6:6–11

This is perhaps the most colorful and instructive of all the passages in Proverbs regarding work. It provides both a positive example to emulate and a negative example to avoid. We begin by considering the positive example, the ant.

"Go to the ant...consider its ways." What an ironic testimony to the extent of our fallen nature! Here the book of Proverbs calls for humanity, the very pinnacle of God's creation, to be instructed by a mindless, soulless, tiny insect. Man, who was placed on the earth to have dominion over all creation, must sit at the feet of the ant to learn a rudimentary lesson on work. Charles Bridges comments on the irony, "Yet what a proof is it of the degradation of the fall, that 'man, created in the image of God,' and made wiser than the creation (Genesis 1:26, Job 35:11), should be sent, as here, to this insignificant school for instruction!"[10] One day, following the Lord's return, we will indeed rule over a new creation with all the diligence, wisdom, effectiveness, and sinlessness God intended for us in Eden. For now, however, our sin nature reduces us to being tutored by a bug.

How does the ant teach us about a biblical work ethic? By displaying an innate and natural desire to work industriously. The ant does not need to be persuaded, browbeaten, or forced to work. This is clearly seen in verses 7–8, which points out that the ant "has no commander, no overseer or ruler, yet it stores its provisions in summer and gathers its food at harvest." Unlike us, the ant does not need some form of accountability to make it work faithfully. Nor does the ant need coaching, pep talks, motivational speakers, or a book chapter on the biblical work ethic. The ant works industriously simply because that is what he was created to do.

And that's exactly the point.

Just like the ant, humanity was also created to work (Genesis 1:28 and 2:15). Yet so often we need a strict work structure or strong incentives imposed on us from outside for us to remain diligent in our work. This proverb calls us to work as we were intended to: For the glory of God, in fulfillment of our purpose here on earth, and not because someone is watching us work or making us work.

The apostle Paul reiterates the substance of this section of the proverb in his epistle to the Colossians, "Slaves, obey your earthly masters in everything; and do it, *not only when their eye is on you* and to win their favor, but with sincerity of heart and reverence for the Lord. *Whatever you do, work at it with all your heart, as working for the Lord, not for men,*" (Colossians 3:22–23, emphasis mine).[11] If we approach our work with the mindset that we are working *for* the Lord, then we will be much more likely to adopt a biblical work ethic and emulate the ant in fulfilling our calling to be industrious laborers in God's world.

Consider the Sluggard

Go to the ant, you sluggard; consider its ways and be wise!

It has no commander, no overseer or ruler, yet it stores its provisions in summer and gathers its food at harvest.

How long will you lie there, you sluggard? When will you get up from your sleep? A little sleep, a little slumber, a little folding of the hands to rest—and poverty will come on you like a bandit and scarcity like an armed man.

Proverbs 6:6–11

After providing the positive example of the ant, this proverb calls us to consider the negative example of the sluggard so that we may avoid his ways. It warns us by illustrating both the nature and consequences of being a sluggard.

First, the proverb unfolds for us the nature of the sluggard. "A little sleep, a little slumber, a little folding of the hands to rest—and poverty will come on you like a bandit and scarcity like an armed man" (vv. 10–11). The sluggard's nature

51

is very clear in the pattern of sleep . . . slumber . . . rest. We all need sleep, but the sluggard doesn't *get* up when he *wakes* up. Instead he stays in bed, slumbering, dreaming. The suggestion here is that he does this not merely once in a while, but regularly and habitually. This habit defines him. In his luxurious slumber he rolls over—back and forth like a door on its hinges, as Proverbs 26:14 puts it—rather than getting up and going about his business. And when he is done slumbering, drifting in and out of dreamland, he *still* doesn't get up! He folds his hands across his chest and lies there, resting and relaxing while the day slips away.

The proverb next turns to the consequences of being a sluggard. In verse 11, the sluggard is warned that "poverty will come on you like a bandit and scarcity like an armed man." Get in the habit of sleep . . . slumber . . . rest—and all the idleness and lack of concern for your work that this suggests—and you are very likely to suffer the hardship of poverty. By choosing not to be diligent the sluggard, in effect, chooses poverty. This cause and effect relationship between idleness and poverty is a major emphasis in the book of Proverbs. There are at least fourteen passages in Proverbs that connect idleness to poverty.[12] Here are just three:

"Laziness brings on deep sleep, and the shiftless man goes hungry" (Proverbs 19:15).

"A sluggard does not plow in season; so at harvest time he looks but finds nothing" (Proverbs 20:4).

"Do not love sleep or you will grow poor; stay awake and you will have food to spare" (Proverbs 20:13).

The sluggard refuses to obey God's call to work diligently, and that embrace of sin has real consequences. While the ant enjoys rich abundance flowing from his labors, the sluggard can find himself in a constant state of want.

In a prosperous society like America, with food in abundance, it is much easier for the sluggard to avoid outright hunger than it was for his Old Testament counterpart. Even by the time of the New Testament, wealth and social organization had advanced to the point that someone who had become poor as a result of being lazy was less likely to go hungry. Yet the lack of diligence displayed by these people, which kept them from being able to supply their own food, was still (and *is* still) a violation of God's purpose that ought not to be tolerated. This was Paul's meaning when he wrote, "For even when we were with you, we gave you this rule: 'If a man will not work, he shall not eat.' We hear that some among you are idle. They are not busy; they are busybodies. Such people we command and urge in the Lord Jesus Christ to settle down and earn the bread they eat" (2 Thessalonians 3:10–12). In other words, there were sluggards in the church taking a free ride.

Certainly there is a place for Christian compassion to the poor (some of the poor are sluggards and some are not), but sluggards *will* become impoverished, and the New Testament teaching regarding sluggards is that any handouts given them ought to be limited and temporary, so that they might repent and become responsible and diligent.

Refusal to embrace a diligent work ethic is sinful because it violates a primary call God has given us as Christians—to echo our Creator who works. The sin of the sluggard (like all sin) has consequences—poverty and want.

Consider Yourself: The Lure of Laziness

When Proverbs 6:6–11 challenges us to consider the ant and the sluggard, it is of course challenging us to consider ourselves. So let's look now at several traits of the sluggard as enumerated in Proverbs 26: 13–16. "The sluggard says, 'There is a lion in the road, a fierce lion roaming the streets!' As a door turns on its hinges, so a sluggard turns on his bed. The sluggard buries his hand in the dish; he is too lazy to bring it back to his mouth. The sluggard is wiser in his own eyes than seven men who answer discreetly." Together these make for a helpful checklist.

The Sluggard Lies and Makes Excuses

There is a lion in the road, a fierce lion roaming the streets!

Proverbs 26:13

This verse indicates colorfully that the sluggard will say all sorts of things, even going to outrageous and ridiculous extremes, to try to avoid work. He will lie to others, misrepresenting reality to try to get out of an unpleasant task. He will lie to himself. He will even admit to himself he is avoiding work, but he will try to suppress his conscience and rationalize it away. I don't personally know anyone who has ever made the excuse given above, but in the absence of lions, our excuses take on equally absurd forms. Two of the most common forms might be called The Exception Excuse, and The Lowest-Common-Denominator Excuse.

The Exception Excuse goes something like this. "I'm entitled to goof off once in a while because . . . I don't make enough money/ I don't get enough vacation/I deserved that promotion last year/This company or my boss make so much money, so how can it possibly matter anyway?" When I make excuses like this, my thought patterns are along the following lines. *I am an exception. I am special, and not like the others. Because I am wise and reasonable, I see a bigger picture than the people who make the rules. In my judgment, the rules aren't exactly fair, so I think I'll just change them a little—as they apply to myself—and not tell anyone.*

It's astonishing how often we are tempted to make the Exception Excuse, with its pitiful rationalizations. Even more astonishing is the arrogance and self-exaltation bound up in our hearts that drives us to make such excuses.

The Lowest-Common-Denominator Excuse essentially takes the opposite approach. This excuse says, "Everyone else is taking it slow. Why not me too?" So the Exception Excuse says, "Because I am *different* from other people, I am justified in being lazy." But the Lowest-Common-Denominator Excuse says, "Because I am *the same* as other people, I am justified in being lazy." It's just another route to the same destination! What ridiculous mental gymnastics we will do to avoid work!

The Sluggard Takes No Initiative

As a door turns on its hinges, so a sluggard turns on his bed.

Proverbs 26:14

A second trait of the sluggard, as noted earlier, is that he shows a serious lack of initiative. The image of the sluggard who won't get out of bed, but rolls back and forth as if he were on hinges, is a vivid one. But in another sense, the door-on-hinges image also depicts someone who moves in a limited range, never making progress. The same simple, unproductive activities are repeated over and over. It's easy and comfortable, so there's no challenge, no growth, no learning, and no real progress. This kind of sluggard does actually perform some work, but he or she never presses forward into something better, more challenging, and more rewarding. Charles Bridges summarizes the sluggard's plight: "as the door upon his hinges, where he was one day, one year, there he is found the next."[13] Getting by on the bare minimum is good enough for this sluggard. Refusing to take initiative, and anchored to a never-changing pattern of minimal exertion, it's easy to see why the sluggard becomes poor.

The Sluggard Does Not Finish His Work

The sluggard buries his hand in the dish; he is too lazy to bring it back to his mouth.

Proverbs 26:15

55

Here again we see a ridiculous example employed to make a point—the sluggard consistently fails to complete his tasks.

How do we engage in this type of behavior? I know how I do it. I allow sinful distractions to lead me away from my work. I allow procrastination to seep into my work habits, delaying difficult or unpleasant tasks for as long as possible. I have left work undone because I knew it would eventually be reassigned to others. At times I can simply give up when the task becomes too challenging.

Can you relate?

The Sluggard is Proud

The sluggard is wiser in his own eyes than seven men who answer discreetly.

Proverbs 26:16

Finally, we come to the root sin of the sluggard. We saw hints of this earlier: The sluggard just considers himself to be smarter than everyone else. He may not express it that way, even to himself. He may have trouble seeing the extent to which this is true. (After all, sin is deceptive so we often don't understand our own motives.) But examine the sluggard's actions, and his true beliefs and motives become clear. At the core of being a sluggard is self-centeredness and self-love, rooted in pride.

Here in verse 16, once again the language is carefully tailored to strengthen and emphasize the central point. The sluggard does not merely see himself as wiser than friends, or peers, or people in general. No, the one who won't get out of bed in the morning or follow the rules at work, the one who lies and makes excuses, the one who won't finish what's begun, thinks himself or herself wiser than "men who answer discreetly." These are men known for the quality and consistency of their judgments. They are the truly wise, yet the sluggard thinks little of their opinion. Even if *seven* such men disagree (the

56

biblical number for perfection being used in this verse very intentionally), the sluggard remains unconvinced.

The sluggard is the "know-it-all" who rejects the counsel of others—their calls to him to leave his bed and get to work, to be diligent and thorough and honor authority, to take on new challenges and not be content with simple tasks. Because of pride, he or she tends to regard others as buffoons and fools, especially bosses, employers, teachers, parents, and other authority figures. Sometimes this takes the form of actual mockery, but it always begins with a heart attitude of dishonor and disrespect—that is, it begins with pride. That dishonor and disrespect is in fact toward God, our true authority and the one who places delegated authority figures in our lives for our good.

Making excuses, doing the bare minimum, failing to complete tasks, and rejecting the counsel of others—this is the composite picture of the sluggard, one of the fools of the book of Proverbs. Being a sluggard is the fool's way of responding to God's call on our lives to be productive and diligent for his glory. The hard-working and industrious person, the person who works hard *for* the Lord, is truly wise, while the foolish sluggard reaps the attendant painful consequences of his or her sin.

Consider Yourself: The Trap of the Workaholic

The sluggard, as we have seen, refuses to embrace God's calling to work diligently. But there is an equal danger at the opposite end of the spectrum: the trap of the workaholic. An honorable, God-glorifying approach to work does not involve a continual obsession with productivity. We are called not only to be workers, but also to be children, spouses, parents, church members, citizens, and stewards of God's material gifts. God's call to us is to have the right heart attitude toward each role, resulting in right priorities.

The Call to be Balanced

Six days you shall labor and do all your work, but the seventh day is a Sabbath to the LORD your God. On it you shall not do any work, neither you, nor your son or daughter, nor your manservant or maidservant, nor your animals, nor the alien within your gates. For in six days the LORD made the heavens and the earth, the sea, and all that is in them, but he rested on the seventh day. Therefore the LORD blessed the Sabbath day and made it holy.

Exodus 20:9–11

You don't have to believe that doing work on the Sabbath is sinful for Christians to recognize that the Fourth Commandment contains much wisdom. God's pattern of creation consisted of work followed by rest. Because God does not need to rest, clearly he was teaching us. This passage establishes in all human life a boundary between work and rest. Many of the tools and institutions of our society may be up and running 24/7, but you and I don't function that way. At the level of the individual, there must be rest—a chosen, intentional respite from productive labor.

To this, the workaholic responds, "You don't understand. How can I possibly stop? There's my family and church and job and friends and possessions. So much to be done . . . if I don't keep going I'll fall behind. I'll fail!" I understand that temptation. In fact, I gave in to it. It's not easy to accept God's call to be balanced. That's why he also gives us the call to reject idolatry, and the call to trust.

The Call to Reject Idolatry

Put to death, therefore, whatever belongs to your earthly nature: sexual immorality, impurity, lust, evil desires and greed, which is idolatry.

Colossians 3:5

We misread this verse if we place too much emphasis on the items at the beginning of this list and minimize those at the end. Lust and evil desires can have as much to do with material greed as they do with sexual immorality. Paul is telling us that unbridled lusts and inordinate affections *of any and all kinds* are inconsistent with the Christian's calling.

Generally, people become workaholics because they covet something—they are so greedy for this something that they have made it into an idol that they worship by consistently giving it more attention than it deserves. Some workaholics covet money, some covet fame, some covet power, some covet mastery of a skill or craft, and some covet *not* attending to other God-ordained responsibilities in their lives. It's possible to covet several or all of these at the same time! Just as with sexual desire, which is also a gift from God, the desire to work can be perverted when it degrades into lust, greed, and idolatry.

The Call to Trust

Unless the LORD builds the house, its builders labor in vain. Unless the LORD watches over the city, the watchmen stand guard in vain. In vain you rise early and stay up late, toiling for food to eat—for he grants sleep to those he loves.

Psalm 127:1–2

No wonder this passage sounds so much like a section of Proverbs. It is from a wisdom Psalm attributed to Solomon, the primary author of Proverbs. But whereas in Proverbs, Solomon goes to some lengths to warn us against the error of the sluggard, here in Psalm 127, he balances that by warning us against the error of those who have a workaholic mindset.

When does our toil become vain? When we detach our work from trust in God. When we seek to wrest control from God and take our lives entirely and exclusively into our own hands. It is the Lord who must build our house. It is the Lord who must watch our city. It is the Lord who must be in all of our labors, or they are pointless. When work becomes my object of worship and devotion, I have embraced vanity, divorced God from my labors, and become an idolater. I have rejected the enduring promise of the Savior who, in speaking to his disciples specifically about worries over material provision, said, "Seek first his kingdom and his righteousness, and all these things will be given to you as well" (Matthew 6:33).

Today, I believe Christians are actually more likely to become workaholics than they are sluggards, simply because the idolatry of workaholism is more socially respectable. In fact, it is so widely praised that many Christians don't even consider it a sin! As a pastor, I certainly became a workaholic . . . and my idolatry won me praise! People often commended me for my ability to multi-task and get things done. I often allowed the boundaries between work and rest to be blurred. There were so many "good things" to do with my time: preach, teach, counsel, discipline, go to the soccer games and plays of the children in my congregation, teach at seminary, teach at college, speak at conferences and write books. In serving "24/7," I was trying to build God's house without his help by shouldering all the responsibilities for his church myself.

In the final analysis, we can stop working and rest because God is sovereign. He is in control, not us. If we are not pursuing his priorities—which include rest as well as a broad range of responsibilities—our efforts will ultimately be futile, no matter how hard we work. But as we embrace a balanced life that includes work, rest, and proper attention to all our responsibilities, he will provide all we need to accomplish his will.

It's extremely liberating to recognize that God gives us enough time to finish everything to which he has actually called us. Here are some of those things: devotional time with God; relationships and service in your family, church, and community; and matters of stewardship over your material goods. If any of these areas are suffering because of the amount of time you spend doing other things, take a close look. Perhaps you are becoming—or became long ago—a workaholic, an idolater who has foolishly dethroned God by believing that his ways, so plainly presented in Scripture, are inferior to your own.

Both Sins the Same

The sin of the sluggard is serious, but so is that of the workaholic. In fact, they are very similar sins. The man or woman who builds all of life around work is every bit as proud and self-centered as the sluggard. At either extreme we worship an idol called "Doing it My Way." Perhaps the Bible spends a lot more time on sluggards and a lot less on anything we would call "workaholism" because the workaholic is really just a variety of sluggard by another name. Both are interested in avoiding responsibilities that don't interest them. The workaholic simply avoids things by a different technique—crowding them out of his calendar. And where the sluggard is sure to suffer economic loss, the workaholic suffers losses that are often more relational than monetary, but nevertheless real, lasting, and painful.

Work, whatever form it may take, is a core activity of each of our lives, taking up most of our waking moments. What a tragedy to despise it like the sluggard, and live for those times when we are not doing it. What a travesty to worship it like the workaholic, as we strive to deify ourselves in our little kingdom; a tiny god over a tiny world, as if we had created that world ourselves, or sustain it ourselves, or even understand its true workings.

Divine Joy: Imitating the God Who Works

> A man can do nothing better than to eat and drink and find satisfaction in his work. This too, I see, is from the hand of God.
>
> Ecclesiastes 2:24

61

In this chapter we have discussed how work is a calling from God, and a primary reason we are even here. In trying to grapple with the influence of sin, we have received warnings against approaching our work as either a sluggard or as a workaholic, and we have seen these as two sides of the same coin. Along the way we have been encouraged to emulate the impressive industry of the ant, and we have been reminded that God gave us a balanced pattern of work and rest, so we might remain dependent upon his grace instead of our own efforts. Now we come to a final encouragement: When work is in its proper place in our lives, we can taste divine joy.

We serve a God who works. He worked in creation, and from that first instant of created time he has guided and directed each molecule and moment, "sustaining all things by his powerful word" (Hebrews 1:3). Truly, "he is before all things, and in him all things hold together" (Colossians 1:17). Jesus obviously worked with extreme and sacrificial diligence during his time on earth, and is even now seated at the Father's right hand, interceding—working—for us (Romans 8:34).

Our God not only works, continually and with perfect effectiveness, he takes pleasure in his labors. Like a great artist, God repeatedly stepped back from the canvas of creation and declared that it was "good." Our Father also takes great pleasure in the unfolding and completion of his glorious plan of redemption, which is "in accordance with his pleasure and will" (Ephesians 1:5).

As we have seen, work was given to humanity as a gift from God before the fall. As with the other pre-fall gifts of marriage—sexuality and rest—God meant for us to take pleasure in our work, just as he does. One of my favorite films is *Chariots of Fire,* which tells the story of 1924 Olympic gold-medalist Eric Liddell. In one scene, Eric is debating with his sister, Jennie, about the value of his running versus his long-term goal of being a missionary in China. Jennie thinks Eric's running is trivial compared to missionary work. Eric replies to her,

"Jennie...you've got to understand. I believe that God made me for a purpose...for China. But he also made me fast, and when I run, I feel his pleasure."

Eric Liddell found great pleasure in running because it was work that God had gifted him to do. When Liddell was running he knew he was pleasing God in his labor. A similar thing is true for all of us who use our gifts to labor in the kingdom of God. Accountants can feel God's pleasure when accounts balance, lawyers can feel God's pleasure when justice is done, mothers can feel God's pleasure when their children are raised in the ways of the Lord, nurses can feel God's pleasure when they heal and alleviate suffering, and teachers can feel God's pleasure when their students learn about God and his creation.

Obviously, no job is an unbroken chain of perfectly joyful moments. Because of the fall work will be, as it says in Genesis, by the sweat of our brow and filled with thorns and thistles. There will be boredom at times, even tedium, and there will be those mornings when the alarm clock goes off and all we want to do is roll over, like a door on its hinges. But what a privilege that, as Christians, work is not merely a task or job, but a gift from God and a calling! When we work we have the opportunity to imitate our Father, the master worker. When we work we have the opportunity to imitate our Lord Jesus Christ, who is still at work for us. No wonder that when our work is well-performed to God's glory it should bring us pleasure!

Begin living the Proverbs-driven life when it comes to your work. Each day seek out those moments when your work strikes that perfect divine note, when your labor resonates with the song of creation, when your labors imitate the character of the God who made you.

4

Jacob Transformed
Integrity in the Marketplace

The man of integrity walks securely, but he who takes crooked paths will be found out. He who winks maliciously causes grief, and a chattering fool comes to ruin.

Proverbs 10:9–10

After thirty years of walking the earth as fully man and fully God, Jesus embarked one day on his final preparations for public ministry. At the Jordan River, as he was baptized by John, the Holy Spirit descended upon him in bodily form. Soon thereafter, driven into the wilderness by his Father, Jesus fasted in solitude for forty days. At the height of his fatigue and isolation, Satan came to tempt him. There, in the same location, were the person of Christ the Son—divine perfection incarnate—and the physical manifestation of sin: pure evil.

Through several temptations the Enemy sought to persuade Jesus to sin, to act like the Devil rather than like God. One momentary yielding by Christ and all would be lost, for then he could no longer be the sinless sacrifice. While each of Satan's temptations are instructive, one of them has particular relevance to this chapter.

But first, another true story.

Throughout the mid-to-late 1990s, Enron Corporation was an apparent paragon of business excellence. Once a simple and stodgy natural-gas pipeline company, Enron had transformed itself into a high-tech powerhouse engaging in such trendy businesses as Internet bandwidth and electronic energy trading. As a result of this stunning transformation, Enron's stock price soared, and the company soon became a darling of Wall Street.

Just one problem. Enron's riches were built on a foundation of deceit. Essentially, the company's top executives had begun keeping two sets of books. Through a variety of "creative" accounting strategies, they were able to defraud Enron's workers, customers, and investors by making the company appear vastly more profitable than it really was. When the fraud was finally revealed it resulted in one of the largest bankruptcies in American history. Thousands of people lost their jobs and their life savings. How ironic that Enron's corporate logo was a crooked "E," for it was the crookedness of upper management that ultimately led to the company's collapse. Due to a lack of business ethics, Enron had imploded.

One might say that the book of Proverbs effectively predicted the collapse of Enron. "The man of integrity walks securely, but he who takes crooked paths will be found out. He who winks maliciously causes grief, and a chattering fool comes to ruin" (Proverbs 10:9–10). This describes well what happened at Enron. The company's top leadership walked a crooked path and were found out. It's not difficult to imagine executives scheming behind closed doors, full of malicious winks and foolish chatter about how they would deceive the entire world. But Enron had build its house upon the sand, and great was its fall. The executives were eventually divested of their ill-gotten wealth and convicted of criminal offenses—chattering fools, come to ruin.

In the wilderness, Satan offered Jesus a similar kind of crooked path. "The devil took him to a very high mountain and showed him all the kingdoms of the world and their splendor. 'All this I will give you,' he said, 'if you will bow down and worship me'" (Matthew 4:8–9). But Jesus already had all those kingdoms, and more, in the form of a promise from his Father. To attain his reward Jesus had work to do and a job to perform: Live a perfect life and die a perfect death as a sacrifice for sin. But Satan was offering Jesus glory without the cross. He wanted him to back out on his agreement with the Father. He wanted him to take a shortcut, to be unethical, to cheat.

In the previous chapter, we learned what it means to have a biblically balanced attitude toward our work, whatever form that work may take in our lives. Here, we'll examine what it means to do our work with full honesty and integrity despite the fact that the world, the flesh—and yes, the Devil—constantly tempt us to cheat. In short, where the previous chapter was about a godly work *ethic* (working hard); this chapter is about godly work *ethics* (working honestly).

Of Weights and Measures

> The LORD abhors dishonest scales, but accurate weights are his delight.
>
> Proverbs 11:1

The book of Proverbs teaches us about work ethics by emphasizing honesty in the marketplace. It does this primarily through a clear, simple example—the use and misuse of weights and measurements. Proverbs 11:1 addresses this subject using two potentially different yet interrelated unethical business practices.

The first is the use of dishonest scales. In the ancient world, the scale was of course a standard tool for weighing goods in order to assign a value. It included two pans dangling from the ends of a pivoting crossbow, much like the "scales of justice" used as a symbol in the American court system. An unethical trader could easily employ several ways to manipulate the scales themselves to enhance his own profit.

The second is the use of inaccurate weights. Proverbs 20:23 says that God hates false weights, but in Proverbs 11:1 the point is made in the opposite way, noting that God delights in accurate weights. An ancient businessman would carry weights with him, supposedly of a standard mass, to help measure the value of the product he was buying or selling. The product would be placed in one pan of the scale and the weight would be placed in the other pan. This was how value was determined. A clever and unscrupulous trader could increase his profit by selecting a weight either slightly heavier (if he were buying) or lighter (if he were selling).[14]

As common as dishonest scales and inaccurate weights must have been in the ancient world, their twenty-first century equivalents are too many to count. After all, man's natural tendency to sin has not changed. Greed can tempt us to seek an unfair advantage whenever we buy or sell. Laziness or malice toward employers can tempt us to cut corners in the quality and quantity of our work. Homemakers, students, and others who certainly work, if not actually for pay, face their own regular temptations to act with a lack of integrity.

Do you see how a failure of diligence and integrity in your work is a "crooked path," the easy and dishonest way out? This is especially clear in the context of an employment contract. If I hire someone to rake the leaves in my yard, I have a right to expect that that person will rake all the leaves that can reasonably be raked. If I hire someone to pull weeds in my garden for one hour, I have a right to expect a full hour of focused weed-pulling. In the same way, if I am being paid to work a particular office job for forty hours a week, I have made a moral commitment actually to be engaged in labor beneficial to my employer for at least that entire forty hours, every week. Anything less is simply the modern equivalent of false weights or a dishonest scale.

God is not distant from the marketplace. "Honest scales and balances are from the LORD; all the weights in the bag are of his making" (Proverbs 16:11). Labor, fruitfulness, trade, and the exchange of goods are part of his creation. Scripture demonstrates repeatedly that God cares deeply about marketplace ethics. To God, unethical business practices are not matters of indifference or mild displeasure. Indeed, he reserves for them his strongest moral outrage. When Proverbs 11:1 says that, "The LORD abhors dishonest scales," the word "abhors" refers to things God finds detestable and sees as abominations. Elsewhere the word is used to condemn improper sacrifices (Exodus 8:26), gross sexual perversion (Leviticus 18:26, Deuteronomy 22:5), and idolatry (Deuteronomy 7:25). But the verse also tells us that God delights in ethical business behavior. Clearly he is not neutral about these things. Integrity in the marketplace delights God. Falsehood provokes his wrath.

This should have a massive impact on how we live our lives. As Christians we must not be dual-minded, pretending that the matters of daily life are disconnected from God and our responsibility to him. God is Lord of all, including the marketplace.

Padding our timecards, shaving a bit off our tithe, puffing up our sale prices, overstating our estimates, cutting corners on our taxes, cheating on a test, doing our work or chores carelessly: how often we are tempted to try to get something for nothing, defraud someone else, misrepresent our productivity, or rig the market in our favor! But God sets a tremendously high standard for us. How can we, as fallen creatures, practice godly ethics in the workplace with any real consistency? What enables our ethics?

The world's answer is to adopt some sort of code of conduct. This approach has spawned countless seminars and white papers and even produced a new profession, the business ethicist. But as Gordon Marino, himself a member of this new professional community, has noted, "You don't need a weatherman to know which way the wind blows, and CEOs do not need a business ethicist to tell them right from wrong. What they need is the character to do the right thing, which is to say, the mettle to avoid the temptation to talk themselves out of their knowledge of right and wrong even if that knowledge lowers their profit margins."[15]

In other words, it all comes down to character. How can sinners like us come to possess such character and integrity? How can our crooked nature be made straight?

Making the Crooked Straight: The Story of Jacob

If there was ever a man who exemplified crookedness, it was Jacob, son of Isaac and grandson of Abraham. Jacob's very name meant "one who supplants," and for much of his life he lived up to it. He was a master at deceptive dealings, a shrewd manipulator of events. The Bible records three striking instances of unethical business dealings in Jacob's adult life, and these against family members.

First, Jacob set up his elder brother Esau in order to cheat him out of his birthright, persuading him to exchange it for a bowl of stew (Genesis 25:29–34). Esau certainly contributed his own sin to this exchange (Hebrews 12:16), but Jacob controlled the timing and circumstances, introduced the idea, and pushed it to completion. He chose a moment when his brother, whom he knew to be an impulsive man, was weak and famished. Only then did Jacob offer Esau the trade: his birthright for a little warm stew; the passing pleasure of a meal for the most valuable thing Esau possessed; a small, immediate benefit at a crushing cost, one that Esau and his descendants would bear forever. Dishonest scales, indeed.

Second, having obtained Esau's birthright, Jacob later sought to acquire the only thing of value remaining to his brother. With encouragement and assistance from his mother, Jacob successfully deceived his own father, then blind and in weak health, in order to receive a final fatherly blessing intended for Esau (Genesis 27:5–17).

Still later in his life, Jacob dealt deceitfully with his father-in-law, Laban (Genesis 30:31–43). In this case Jacob was able to vastly increase his herd of sheep through trickery, manipulation, and deception, to Laban's considerable financial loss. Much like some modern stock-market scheme, Jacob in effect rigged the market so that he would be certain to gain and Laban would be certain to lose, all the while making it look like the results had been produced entirely by outside forces.

Jacob got something for nothing by stealing his brother's birthright. He received his father's blessing through fraud. And he rigged the livestock market in order to cheat Laban and prosper himself. His entire life had been marked by lies, fraud, and deceit. Clearly, this was a man who gloried in cheating others for his own benefit.

All the more amazing, then, that we see Jacob, later in life, as a new man—a man of honesty, integrity, and principle—a supplanter no longer. What happened to Jacob? What changed a lifelong fraud into a man of honor? Of more immediate significance, what can change you and me? What can cause us to turn away from the grasping and greediness that often fills our hearts and underlies our every act of fraud, whether great or small?

Let us briefly examine Jacob's transformation, that we too might learn how to change.

Jacob Transformed

When Jacob was very old, the region of Canaan suffered a famine so severe that Jacob had to send his sons to Egypt to buy grain (Genesis 42–43), a round trip of some 500 miles. Previously in Genesis, we learn that Jacob's sons had much earlier sold their brother Joseph into slavery. Joseph had ended up in Egypt, and by the time of the famine had risen to a position of great political power. Ironically, when Jacob's sons then came to Egypt in weakness and humility, they unknowingly dealt with their own brother.

Joseph recognized his siblings but did not let on. He provided them with grain, but instructed his servants to place the money his brothers used to buy the grain secretly back in their sacks. When the brothers returned home and Jacob learned that he had both the grain and the silver, we might expect him to have said something like, "Great job, boys! You're all chips off the old block!" But this man, who had three times gone out of his way to steal from his own family, had a very different reaction. He sent his sons on another 500-mile journey to Egypt, telling them, "Take double the amount of silver with you, for you must return the silver that was put back into the mouths of your sacks. Perhaps it was a mistake" (Genesis 43:12).

The situation was somewhat more complicated than I have described here. As you can see in Genesis 42–43, Jacob was also concerned about the fact that Joseph had kept one son, Simeon, in Egypt, and demanded to see the youngest son, Benjamin, who had not been on the journey. Nevertheless, in Jacob's response to the returned silver there is not a hint of grasping or scheming to keep it. Instead, we see a man unwilling to deceive. Once a liar and cheater, now he refuses to engage in unethical business practices, even when the opportunity falls into his lap. He will not seek something for nothing, defraud another, or rig the market in his favor. And it is all due to an encounter with the living God.

Jacob Wrestles with God

Between the account of Jacob defrauding Laban, and the time of Jacob's honest dealing with Egypt, the Supplanter experiences a transformational event: In Genesis 32, he wrestles all night with the living God. What a picture of Jacob's stubborn, unyielding nature (and our own) and the relentless, loving efforts that God exerts to humble and transform every child of his who goes astray!

During this night of wrestling, God changes Jacob's name to Israel. At the time, Jacob was actually in flight from Laban and Laban's sons, who had become angry at the way Jacob had prospered at Laban's expense. This transformation, exemplified by Jacob's name-change, was an act of God that came close on the heels of Jacob's serious sin.

To have your name changed by God is to have your destiny altered. Elsewhere in the Bible when God changes someone's name, often it is simply a modification, such as Abram's name becoming Abraham and Sarai's becoming Sarah. Other times it reflects a radical change in one's nature. That was certainly the case with Jacob. That night, the transforming grace of God came upon the liar and cheater, Jacob. That man, after whose sons the twelve tribes of Israel would be named, now bore a name with El – a reference to God – woven right into it. "Jacob" no longer, now he was Israel, a man with the integrity to go out of his way to make good on a financial transaction that had appeared to grant him an unjust windfall.

What birthed these new-found principles in the man Israel? What inspired him to act on them in the moment of testing? Was it a commitment to a code of conduct or to sound business ethics? A determination to "do the right thing"? No. It was the transforming grace of God. That alone is what enabled the ethics of Jacob-turned-Israel.

You and I are not so different from Jacob. You see, God had much earlier promised to *give* Jacob the very things Jacob spent his life trying to *steal*. God told Jacob that he would prosper and that his older brother Esau would eventually serve him. At Jacob's birth, it was declared that the "older would serve the younger" (Genesis 25:23). All along, *Jacob was destined to have the birthright and blessing.* But that which God had promised to freely give him, Jacob tried to seize through deceit and fraud, pursuing a holy blessing by sinful means.

Jacob's sin was not his desire to acquire these things. After all, God had promised them to him. Rather, his sin was in attempting to gain the blessing through his own unethical ways.

Jacob's Promises, and Ours

God promised to give specific things to Jacob, yet Jacob spent much of his life trying to steal those things. What has God promised you, and me, and every one of his children? Let's recall just a few of his promises.

1. He will never leave us or forsake us (Hebrews 13:5).
2. He makes all things work together for our good (Romans 8:28).
3. He provides all that we need (Matthew 6:31–33, 2 Corinthians 9:8).
4. He will bring us safely to heaven (John 14:2–3).

Here are four promises from Scripture—merely the briefest overview of God's explicit, personal, spoken commitment to each of us. (Indeed, the entire Bible tells the story of God's unending faithfulness to do good to his children!) But in just these four, we have promises far more wonderful than the promises God made to Jacob. What is getting the birthright compared to these?

Surely we can't make any of these things happen on our own. We can't make God be faithful to us (the first promise in the list) or bring us to heaven (the last promise in the list). But neither of those promises are the main focus of this chapter, anyway. Our topic here is ethics, which places our attention on promises two and three. You and I behave unethically—we sin—when we believe that by doing the right thing we will *fail to get* either something that's good for us (promise two) or something we need (promise three). *That* is where our ethics are tested.

God's unbreakable commitment to us includes a promise to work all things for our good, and to provide all we need. Our proper response to those promises is to do our work (or school or child-rearing or athletic training or anything else) with our best efforts (Ecclesiastes 9:10) and to the glory of God (1 Corinthians 10:31). Then we leave the rest up to him. He initiates the promises in mercy and love; we obey the promises in faith; and he fulfills the promises by grace, at the right time and in the right way.

Do I rest consistently in those promises? Do I go through each day confident that it is by God's grace alone they will be fulfilled? Or, like Jacob, do I strive sinfully to bring them about under my own power? Do I hedge my bets? Do I think maybe God won't mind if I grab something other than what he intends for me to have? Do I try to obtain something sooner than he would give it to me in his sovereign, perfect timing?

In answering these questions, none of us can claim to be blameless. So much of our sin is simply an effort to gain by sinful means the satisfaction or security that God has promised to give us freely. (Make no mistake—all our grasping, selfish, Jacob-like sins are among those for which Christ died, and his forgiveness is freely available.) And the Bible doesn't suggest that, even after Jacob's wrestling match with God, he never again sinned in this way, either. But we do see a man who had come to a new and far deeper understanding of what it means to walk in trust. We too can gain a greater reliance on God's goodness and faithfulness in these areas and as a result grow in our ability to resist temptation.

When Jesus was in the wilderness, Satan was essentially offering him a measly bowl of stew—a false, premature version of God's promised best—in exchange for his birthright.

Jesus refused the temptation to shortcut God's plan and take matters into his own hands. He did not hold his birthright in contempt, but stood unyieldingly on the Word of God.

For us to grow in resisting temptation we need, just like Jacob, to have a transforming encounter with the living God—with Jesus, our Redeemer, the only one who has never been unethical in his dealings. Our wrestling with God takes place through his Word, mediated by the indwelling Holy Spirit. As we come before God and engage honestly and completely, we leave changed, our pride and self-sufficiency hobbled, our perspective altered. So let us not resist God when he seeks—through his Word, through preaching of the Scriptures, through the counsel of a friend—to wrestle our pride to the ground. By his grace, he can ready us to resist the temptation to take into our own hands the fulfillment of God's perfect promises.

God must take our crooked inclinations and make them straight. His saving and sanctifying grace must enable and empower our ethics. Then, when tempted to try to shortcut God's promises, we can do as our Savior did in the desert: Stand unyieldingly on the perfect promises found in the Word of God. God has promised to work all things for our good, and to give us all that we need. In light of this, what cause is there for unethical dealings in business or any other area of life? None. Our lives are but a vapor, but our God is eternal, holy, sovereign, and good—how futile and counterproductive for us to try to seize control back from him! Let us trust him, work diligently and honesty, then marvel at his goodness and thank him for his provision. In the area of ethics, this is how we are empowered to live a Proverbs-driven life.

PART THREE

Wealth

A Proverbs-Driven Life understands the place and purpose of material wealth.

5

Biblical Prosperity

Seeking Wealth with the Right Heart

Everyone also to whom God has given wealth and possessions and power to enjoy them, and to accept his lot and
rejoice in his toil—this is the gift of God.

Ecclesiastes 5:19

---

*M*ost of us pay at least some attention to our health.
We hardly have a choice. Health advice is everywhere! The
latest exercises and dieting fads demand our unquestioned
acceptance. We are constantly encouraged to eat lots of some
foods and very little of others. And apparently we are all supposed to drink more water each day than our grandparents
drank in a fortnight.

Yes, we like the idea of better health. We might even be
willing to sacrifice and change some of our habits to become
healthier. But as we mentally lace up our jogging shoes and
stand poised to hit the health track, we notice it has all these
twists and turns. In several places it doubles back on itself and

appears to be full of detours and dead ends. But really, how could it be a smooth, clear path? After all, the health experts keep changing their minds!

For example, throughout most of my life, eating eggs on a regular basis was considered unhealthy. Then one day the doctors announced that, well, maybe they had been wrong about that. Similarly, margarine was promoted by the medical establishment to save us from the evils of butter. That was unquestioned truth for decades. But now? Perhaps margarine isn't so great for you after all. Coffee was once seen as nothing but a harmful vice, yet today the experts say it probably has some health benefits. So, one minute a particular food is to be avoided, and the next minute it is to be embraced. What are we supposed to believe?

Something similar can happen when we review what the Bible has to say about wealth. On the one hand, Scripture warns us strongly against the dangers of wealth. The rich, after all, are the bad guys in many biblical accounts and are frequently reprimanded or condemned. Commands against coveting seem to denounce even the desire for wealth. Then, just when you're becoming convinced that wealth ought to be avoided, you read a passage extolling its virtues. God seems to grant some people great wealth and it's called a blessing! Abraham becomes very wealthy. Israel leaves Egypt with vast possessions. The treasuries of David and Solomon overflow. Proverbs commends the diligent acquisition of wealth. What are we to make of all this? Is wealth good or bad? Is it to be embraced or avoided?

At times like this, it's best to look through the lens of God's wisdom in order to gain a proper, biblical understanding of wealth. That's why we're taking two chapters to examine the subject. In this chapter we will discuss how to think about wealth, and in the next chapter we will discuss how to use it.

Wealth and the Human Heart

Millions of people who know very little about the Bible are nevertheless pretty sure that, somewhere in that big book, there is something about money being "the root of all evil." While that phrase may be stuck in the popular consciousness as a carry-over from the King James translation of 1 Timothy 6:10, reliable modern translations render the verse with a more nuanced meaning: "love of money is a root of all kinds [or all sorts] of evil." The first thing to see here is that money is not the basic problem at all, but rather our love for it.

This means that money is not inherently evil. Indeed, in itself wealth is morally neutral; neither good nor bad. The moral issues regarding wealth arise entirely from how we acquire it, relate to it, and use it. In other words, the problem is us. In the final analysis, the Bible teaches that money and material prosperity are actually gifts from God, as shown in Ecclesiastes 5:19 at the beginning of this chapter: "Everyone also to whom God has given wealth and possessions and power to enjoy them, and to accept his lot and rejoice in his toil—this is the gift of God."

Of course, just as with the gift of human sexuality, what we do with that gift isn't always good. This is not a reflection on the gift but on the one who uses it. As sinners, we have an astonishing capacity to bring the corruption of our sin nature to bear on anything we touch. It's true that money does present us with unique temptations, as we will soon discuss. It buys us stuff and makes us feel important. Yet the evil comes not from money but from our coveting hearts. It is because of who we are, not because of what money is, that prosperity can so easily become an object of worship.

So, wealth is ultimately what we make it—but the challenge is that in our sin we have a strong tendency to make it an idol. We forget that for all its ability to give us power and possessions, wealth has unchangeable, permanent, insurmountable limitations. Let's review those limitations, and then look at how we should evaluate the process of gaining wealth.

The Limitations of Wealth

Wealth is arguably the secular religion of the modern Western world. Although it was a good and noble idea to print "In God We Trust" on U.S dollars, the irony is that most Americans trust in their finances far more than in their Creator. For them money is, in effect, the focus of their worship and devotion. Yet Proverbs counsels us to remember that money isn't everything. In fact, money is a poor source of happiness, a rich source of temptation and, in the final analysis, completely worthless.

Wealth is a Poor Source of Happiness

Blessed is the man who finds wisdom, the man who gains understanding, for she is more profitable than silver and yields better returns than gold.

Proverbs 3:13–14

From our man-centered perspective, it is natural to see material wealth as a way of attaining desirable things. That is why people so readily build their lives around it. But Scripture answers the question, "How do I attain desirable things?" from a *God*-centered perspective that puts wealth in a whole new light.

Taken in isolation, the passage above from Proverbs 3 can seem to suggest that wisdom and wealth are at odds with one another. But of the relationship between wealth and wisdom, it's important that we understand what Proverbs is and is not saying. As we keep reading in Proverbs 3, we come to this: "Long life is in her [wisdom's] right hand; in her left hand are riches and honor. Her ways are pleasant ways, and all her paths are peace" (vv. 16–17). Do you see the promise here? As Bruce Waltke puts it, "Wisdom has inestimable superiority to precious metals because it bestows *spiritual virtues* along with material benefits" (emphasis mine).[16] The wisdom that comes from God positions you to enjoy a life that is long, pleasant, peaceful, honorable, *and* materially prosperous.

This passage, and others from Proverbs, teaches that by seeking God's wisdom you *will* gain wealth, but you will *also* gain long life, honor, and peaceful, pleasant ways. This tells us that the wealth attained through prizing and applying God's wisdom is ultimately *more satisfying* than the wealth attained by prizing and applying our own wisdom. Both approaches can be profitable to a degree. Both can yield material returns. But to seek God's wisdom is to attain wealth in a much more satisfying form.

Will your bank account necessarily be a great deal larger if you pursue God's wisdom? No, that's not what Scripture teaches at all. That would be to affirm that the amassing of wealth is the way to happiness. It is not. Pursued apart from God's wisdom, the amassing of wealth is a path of foolishness. Instead, true satisfaction lies in seeking to live by God's wisdom in all your ways. As we do this, we find whatever level of wealth we need 1) to be truly satisfied and 2) to carry out our calling in God.

The world can certainly give you a shallow, material happiness. But only God can give you wisdom leading to a life that is deeply satisfying. The exclusive pursuit of material wealth is therefore a false route, the wrong means to the end. Get godly wisdom and you will be less compelled by the pull of mere money, and you will be able to enjoy God's riches at a far deeper level, freely receiving blessings and spiritual riches that cannot be purchased.

Wealth is a Rich Source of Temptation

Better a poor man whose walk is blameless than a rich man whose ways are perverse.

Proverbs 28:6

83

A second limitation of wealth, as we have already mentioned, is how easily we set our hearts on it, which in turn draws us into sin. In writing to Timothy, Paul recalls how he has seen the love of money bring grief and disillusionment to Christians, even causing them to wander from their faith in God. "For the love of money is a root of all kinds of evil. Some people, eager for money, have wandered from the faith and pierced themselves with many griefs" (1 Timothy 6:10). As we read Paul's warning, and witness the ungodly worship of riches all around us, we must admit that wealth is an easy path to serious spiritual problems. No wonder, then, that Scripture often portrays the rich as morally corrupt.

The danger is two-fold. First, wealth can appear so attractive that we come to believe it should be obtained at all costs. This false belief draws us into a lifestyle that is unwise or outright sinful. Once convinced that the ends justify the means, it is a small step to throw off moral restraints, embrace greed, and come to worship wealth and its pursuit.

A huge proportion of crimes, from pickpocketing to complex corporate skullduggery, are rooted in the sin of greed. We allow dollar signs to blind our eyes to what is right. Fraud, embezzlement, counterfeiting, larceny, shoplifting, drug trafficking, armed robbery, tax evasion, and toxic dumping are just some of the more obvious crimes fueled, in whole or in part, by unfettered desire for money.

Far more common and ultimately more damaging than criminality is simple imbalance. Intense concern with more and more wealth can easily result in a lifestyle characterized by prolonged obsession with work and extended isolation from others. Married people begin ignoring spouses and children. Single people begin living in social shells. Church members neglect meetings and relationships. And money quickly proves to be a poor friend and a worse counselor.

Second, because riches grant us a measure of independence and social power, the wealthy can be tempted to pride, arrogance, self-sufficiency, and self-indulgence. Ironically, for a surprisingly large number of people, merely *pretending* to be wealthy can tempt them to the very same sins.

The perverse ways of the rich noted in Proverbs 28:6 can include self-centeredness, self-indulgence, idolatry, and outright criminality. Truly, the love of money is a root of all kinds of evil.

Wealth is Ultimately Worthless

Wealth is worthless in the day of wrath . . .

Proverbs 11:4

Material wealth is of this world, and cannot last beyond this world (see Luke 12:15–21). Thus, as a third limitation, its value is temporary. For each of us, worldly riches will at some point prove to be entirely worthless.

In this life, in the normal course of events, material riches can be lost to crime, physical deterioration, expenses, or economic downturns. As Jesus admonished us, "Do not store up for yourselves treasures on earth, where moth and rust destroy, and where thieves break in and steal. But store up for yourselves treasures in heaven, where moth and rust do not destroy, and where thieves do not break in and steal. For where your treasure is, there your heart will be also" (Matthew 6:19). Again, in perfect accord with the overall biblical teaching on wealth, note that Jesus' warning is against *setting your heart* on riches. The problem is never money itself, but always our love of money.

Then, whatever wealth you or I may still possess on the day we die or the day Christ returns, it will at that moment prove utterly and completely worthless. Ezekiel provides a sobering elaboration on the point made in Proverbs 11:4, "They will throw their silver into the streets, and their gold will be an unclean thing. Their silver and gold will not be able to save them in the day of the LORD's wrath. They will not satisfy their hunger or fill their stomachs with it, for it has made them stumble into sin" (Ezekiel 7:19). Men and women who have worshiped riches will one day find themselves tragically betrayed: Their god has no power to save.

God's Get-Rich-Slow Scheme

So far in this chapter we have reviewed the dangers and limitations of wealth, and we have seen that despite these potential pitfalls neither wealth nor its pursuit are inherently wrong. Armed with that understanding, we can now discuss the biblical approach to acquiring wealth. For indeed, the pursuit of material wealth can be entirely godly, and producing wealth is certainly central to the divine calling of a great many Christians. Where Scripture differs from much of human wisdom in this regard, however, is in teaching that wealth ought to be gained gradually, and with the proper heart attitude. Simply stated, the Bible teaches us that the best way to get rich is to do be willing to do so slowly, intentionally, and in reliance on God.

The Foolishness of Financial Haste

The plans of the diligent lead to profit as surely as haste leads to poverty.

Proverbs 21:5

"Earn up to $25,000 a month while staying at home." "Make millions in real estate with no money down." "Play the lottery and win instantly." Mantras like these regularly assault our eyes and ears. The appeal of gaining wealth quickly and easily can be very powerful. An endless supply of opportunists and charlatans are ever eager to sell the latest repackaged get-rich-quick scheme to an equally endless supply of what the Bible calls fools. And no matter how wisely you and I behaved yesterday, or for the past fifteen years, we could easily be tempted by foolishness today. Never imagine you have become too spiritually mature to play the fool; that would be to imagine you are no longer capable of sin.

The book of Proverbs warns us against all notions of easy wealth, and depicts financial haste as foolish for two reasons. First, it is sinful. And secondly, it simply doesn't work.

When Proverbs 28:20 tells us that, "A faithful man will be richly blessed, but one eager to get rich will not go unpunished," it depicts those "eager to get rich" as unfaithful to God. In their eagerness for easy wealth, they display financial haste through some or all of the following sins: greediness, laziness, lack of faith, self-reliance, fraud, and impatience.

This verse goes on to state that the sins of financial haste (like all sins) will be punished. Such punishment may come in a variety of forms. It may include the collapse and failure of the get-rich-quick scheme that has become an idol. It may also involve any profits gained from a dishonest endeavor ultimately proving to be of little lasting value. As Proverbs 13:11 puts it, "Dishonest money dwindles away." How many get-rich-quick schemes use dishonest tactics like multi-leveling marketing to deceive people into believing they can get rich in haste?

This leads us to the second reason financial haste is foolish: It doesn't work. Perhaps the most common sin associated with financial haste is laziness. The lazy person is thrilled to find some sort of financial trick that caters to his or her sin, one that promises great returns for very little effort. But we see in Proverbs 10:4 that, "Lazy hands make a man poor, but diligent hands bring wealth," while Proverbs 21:5 assures us that, "haste leads to poverty."

Is it possible to make a lot of money rapidly and legitimately through wisdom, skill, and timing? On rare occasions, yes it is. And to find yourself positioned for such gain is not a bad thing. As long as your heart is right, Scripture does not obligate you to refuse the opportunity. But to build your strategy of wealth acquisition around seeking to capitalize on these rare events—to run after them passionately as the gambler does his next lottery ticket or trip to the blackjack table—reveals a heart of greed and financial haste, which Scripture does denounce. Let these episodes be the exception and gradual wealth accumulation the primary goal and attitude.

The Wisdom of Financial Diligence

Dishonest money dwindles away, but he who gathers money little by little makes it grow.

Proverbs 13:11

In many places, Scripture defines the virtuous approach to gaining wealth in the negative, that is, by describing what marks its opposite. But where Scripture defines it positively— and a typical approach in Proverbs is to contrast a negative example with a positive—one concept stands out: diligence. In fact, as we have already seen, diligence and laziness are frequently contrasted in Proverbs. Throughout Scripture, diligence is associated with wisdom and wealth, and laziness with foolishness and poverty. In this section we will focus on Proverbs 13:11, where the diligence of gathering money "little by little" is commended.

The Bible teaches that God has embedded his comprehensive norms and laws into the very fabric of creation. For example, in one sense biology is simply the ongoing discovery of God's laws as they apply to living things, while the study of chemistry uncovers God's laws as they apply to the natural elements. Similarly, there is a set of unchanging divine laws regarding the creation and use of wealth. Clearly, in financial matters the "little by little" approach of diligence is an expression of this divine economic wisdom.

The gradual growth in wealth brought about by diligence can be seen in operation at various levels. At a simple level, faithfulness in performing a paid job brings in money gradually but steadily. When rightly managed, savings from a regular income can grow considerably over time. A more dramatic example, however, can be seen in the principle of compound interest. It is said that Albert Einstein once referred to compound interest as the greatest mathematical discovery of all time. Here is an example of compounding that is simple yet powerful.

If you had a piece of paper large enough to fold in half fifty times (and if you could actually, physically, fold it that many times) how high would it reach? Several feet? Two stories? To the highest treetops? How about a mile? *Ten* miles? Remember, every time you fold it, you double the previous thickness. Folding a piece of paper of average thickness fifty times would therefore produce a tower *more than 70 million miles high!*

That is the utterly astonishing power of compounding. Now, money cannot be compounded at the same rate paper is folded. Every fold increases the previous thickness by 100 percent, and in practical terms financial investments tend to grow, not at 100 percent a year, but more like 5 percent to 10 percent a year. Still, some remarkable gains can be made by such investments over the long term. Here's how it works.

When you invest money in, for example, a government bond, in the first year you earn interest on the money you have invested (your capital). The second year you earn interest on your capital plus the interest earned in the first year. The third year you earn interest on your capital plus the interest earned in the first two years. (You get the idea.) This pattern of earning interest on your interest is called compounding. Like repeatedly folding a piece of paper, or rolling a snowball down a hill in fresh snow, the longer your investment has been compounding, the faster it grows.

If you start from nothing, and put $2,000 a year into an investment that pays 8 percent interest, in thirty years you will have invested $60,000. But your investment will be *worth* approximately $245,000. This means your $60,000 has produced an additional $185,000 with absolutely no effort on your part…except for diligence, faithfulness, and patience. Diligence, faithfulness, and patience, that is, to keep earning money consistently…to maintain a lifestyle that consumes less money than you earn…to take that extra money and regularly add it to an investment that earns steady interest….and to resist the temptation to take any money out of that investment except for the purpose for which it was created (retirement, purchase of a home, college, etc.).

In the New Testament, Jesus himself commends and even commands a heart of diligence and fruitfulness. He does this through the Parable of the Ten Minas (Luke 19:11–27). In the parable, a nobleman planning to leave town for a while calls ten of his servants together. He gives each servant the same sum of money and directs each to invest it until he returns. Upon his return, he judges their investments. The nobleman is very pleased with the first servant, for he has earned a tenfold increase on the sum entrusted to him. This servant is thus rewarded with even greater resources and responsibilities. The second servant has earned a fivefold increase. With this the nobleman is again very pleased, and the servant is rewarded. The third servant, however, returns to the nobleman the exact sum with which he had been originally entrusted. Deeply displeased, the nobleman takes the money from that third servant and entrusts it to the first.

While this parable does pertain to money and economics, it is primarily about the kingdom of God. It strongly urges all Christians to invest the gifts, talents, and opportunities God has entrusted to us to increase God's kingdom and glory, as we anticipate the return of our Lord and Savior. But let us also note how Jesus chooses to illustrate this vital spiritual reality. He is not just telling a nice story. Nor is he describing a fantasy world that operates by laws different from our own. He is setting this parable in a comprehensible, believable reality, one that operates by processes we recognize and understand. He is, in fact, employing a true economic principle grounded in the basic laws by which he, as Creator, has ordered creation.

Diligence produces wealth, a little at first, then more over time. The more wealth that is acquired, the better the diligent person is positioned for further increase, in turn creating additional opportunities for growth. And on it goes, compounding and compounding. This economic reality echoes spiritual reality, for even the laws of everyday economics are based in God's laws. An economically wise person will gather money little by little in an investment account. A person who understands God's wisdom in the larger sense will use that same principal of compounding and "invest" their "spiritual resources" in God's kingdom, where the rewards are unfading and eternal.

A Proverbs-driven life will include the diligent and systematic investment of wealth, but it will do so as part of a larger understanding that we are called to diligently and systematically invest *every* aspect of our lives into the kingdom of our God and Savior. In matters both material and spiritual, the principle of compound growth is woven into creation. The book of Proverbs is particularly addressed to the young (Proverbs 1:4) because the sooner one understands these things and gets on the path to biblical wisdom, the better.

Finally, building wealth gradually is wise because it allows us to better manage the temptations and responsibilities of prosperity. Wealth that comes upon a person quickly can have devastating results. The lives of lottery winners, for example, are often harmed by sudden riches, sometimes severely. Ill-equipped to handle a flood of cash, big-time lottery winners often engage in wasteful spending or fall victim to unwise counsel. Broken relationships, divorce, and even bankruptcy are among the tragic but not unusual outcomes.

This should come as no surprise. The more abruptly and strongly a new temptation or role comes upon us, the more likely we are to struggle or fail. We see this principle at work in a wisdom Psalm of David: "Therefore let everyone who is

91

godly pray to you while you may be found; surely when the mighty waters rise, they will not reach him" (Psalm 32:6). Too much temptation or responsibility, too quickly, is like being swept away by a raging river. But when you get rich slowly, according to the paradigm of Proverbs, you and your money can mature together, so to speak. Gathering money "little by little" makes it far easier to use that money wisely, generously, and biblically.

Wealth has its limitations. A wise person remembers that money can never be the top priority in life, that money can become a source of great temptation, and that money has only temporal value. A truly wise person realizes that his true wealth is found in being a co-heir with Jesus Christ (Romans 8:17). This type of wealth will never perish, spoil, or fade (1 Peter 1:4). Those who are truly wise will find their wealth and inheritance in the riches of knowing Jesus.

Neither Poverty Nor Riches

> Keep falsehood and lies far from me; give me neither poverty nor riches, but give me only my daily bread. Otherwise, I may have too much and disown you and say, "Who is the LORD?" Or I may become poor and steal, and so dishonor the name of my God.
>
> Proverbs 30:8–9

In the end, Proverbs teaches us that acquiring wealth is a blessing, but one that comes with practical and moral risks. If we are informed by and attentive to wealth's dangers and limitations, it is possible to acquire wealth virtuously and with relative safety.

But how much is enough? How much is too much? Of course, there are no numbers one can cite that would apply to all circumstances. "Daily bread" will mean vastly different things for different people. Depending on one's calling, responsibilities, and surrounding culture, one person's riches will be another person's poverty. This is why the Bible directs us to watch carefully our covetous hearts. It is not a matter of how much wealth we have but how we relate to it and (as we will see in the next chapter) what we do with it.

This is where the attitude toward wealth seen in Proverbs 30:8–9 becomes invaluable. This passage captures well the heart of a wise man in regard to wealth: Give me neither poverty nor riches. In this way we find our true wealth, and place our ultimate trust, in God alone. Contentment in daily bread and in Jesus, the true bread from heaven (John 6:32) —in these, we have riches eternal.

6

Financial Stewardship

Using Wealth for the Right Purposes

Honor the LORD with your wealth.
Proverbs 3:9

---

*G*reed is good." This was the motto of the fictional financial mogul Gordon Gekko, played by Michael Douglas in the 1987 film, *Wall Street.* The movie tried to capture the essence of American life in the 1980s, often referred to as the "Me Decade." While the '80s may be history, that era's headlong rush into materialism is still with us. Modern Western culture, fueled by a largely amoral free-market capitalism, has made the care and feeding of personal greed a permanent cultural obsession.

This second chapter on wealth is therefore intended to help us reject the advice of Gordon Gekko and embrace the financial wisdom of Proverbs. The goal is that we would learn to use our finances rightly—under the authority of Scripture and the Lordship of Christ, for the glory of God. Where the last chapter helped us form a biblical attitude toward wealth and its acquisition, this chapter instructs us how to apply what we have learned: how to, in Solomon's words, "Honor the Lord with your wealth."

Let's examine the context of that phrase for a moment. The words were written with the Old Testament system of sacrifice in mind. When we consider that system today we tend to focus on a few of the more vivid aspects, such as slaughtered animals and the smoke of offerings. It's easy to lose sight of the simple human fact that the Israelites who gave animals and crops to God were giving up wealth, genuine economic riches, the very currency of their own survival. Handing over an animal to be *physically* sacrificed was a painful *economic* sacrifice.

Of course, the most important purpose of the Old Testament sacrifices was to offer atonement for sins. For Christians, atonement has been accomplished once and for all by Christ. So while no further sacrifice *for sins* is necessary, Christians are still called to make sacrifices to God as acts of worship. What is the purpose of sacrifices today that are specifically economic in nature? When we set aside the finished issue of atonement, two Old Testament purposes remain in force. We are called to offer to God a meaningful portion of our economic livelihood, 1) to keep us reliant on God and not on riches, and 2) to support those who have been called to serve God's people in specific biblical roles.

Regarding that second point, this chapter is written in the belief that the local church is the primary institutional manifestation of God's work in the world today, just as were the priests and the tabernacle (and later the temple) under the Old Covenant. Therefore, just as Old Testament offerings supported the priests and their work, financial offerings under the New Covenant are intended first and foremost to support pastors, church staff, and church property. While it is beyond the scope of this book to elaborate the reasons, this is the clear teaching of Scripture. Many parachurch ministries may also be worthy of support, but it is the obligation of every Christian to support financially his or her local church before supporting any other ministry.

God has always used the wealth of his people to fund his work. The exchange of goods and services, whether by barter or the use of money, is simply part of how God's creation functions, and the church is no exception. If, as a general rule, we expect God to operate within the *physical* laws, it should be no surprise that he operates also within the *economic* laws, for all such laws are his. This means that God uses money and the workings of the economy to help accomplish his purposes. Some of that money he chooses to get from you and me as we voluntarily, regularly, thankfully, and cheerfully devote a portion of our material prosperity directly to his purposes. As we do so we fund his work, and in giving our money away we fight against our constant tendency to set our hope on riches.

So this chapter is concerned with questions such as the following: *What does Scripture, and the wisdom of Proverbs in particular, teach us that money is for? Now that we hold a biblical understanding of the true nature of wealth, what are we supposed to do with it? How can we be good stewards of whatever wealth God entrusts to us?* In seeking to answer these questions we will discuss four principles that appear to emerge from the overarching command to honor God with our wealth: offer him our "firstfruits"; extend mercy to the poor; be good stewards of what he gives us; live according to our means, and leave an inheritance.

Firstfruits in the 21ˢᵗ Century

Honor the Lᴏʀᴅ with your wealth, [and] **with the firstfruits of all your crops.**

Proverbs 3:9

96

In this verse we find essential guidance for using material wealth biblically. Here, "honor" means to acknowledge God's weightiness, significance, and importance through our words and conduct. Most translations insert an "and" in the middle of the verse, as shown above, separating it into two commands.

This requirement to honor the Lord with our wealth is the foundational principle of wise financial stewardship, and in the second part of verse 9, above, we find the first application of that principle. We are called to honor God—to display his significance in our lives—by offering him "the firstfruits of all [our] crops." In our modern economy, this is perhaps best understood as involving matters of priority and sacrifice.

Give as a Matter of Priority

The principle of giving firstfruits to God began as a response to God's redemption of Israel from the hands of the Egyptians. Consider the words of Deuteronomy 26:8–10:

> "So the LORD brought us out of Egypt with a mighty hand and an outstretched arm, with great terror and with miraculous signs and wonders. He brought us to this place and gave us this land, a land flowing with milk and honey; and now I bring the firstfruits of the soil that you, O LORD, have given me." Place the basket before the LORD your God and bow down before him.

Because God had saved the Israelites from their bondage in Egypt and brought them into the Promised Land, they presented him with sacrificial offerings. Similarly, when we give the "firstfruits" of our wealth to God, we are expressing gratitude for our deliverance from the bondage of sin through the work of Jesus Christ. Honoring God with the firstfruits of our wealth is an act of worship by which we offer thanks for our redemption.

For the ancient Israelite, honoring the Lord with firstfruits meant giving to God the first part of the harvest. This is similar to other Old Testament requirements to offer God the firstborn of the flock or the best of the herd. Today, however, no one dollar of income is better or more valuable than another. In that sense, there is no "best" for us to give. Moreover, wealth tends to flow to us fairly regularly (e.g., in a paycheck) rather than occasionally as it would in an agrarian economy.

Therefore, in the twenty-first century, honoring God with our firstfruits means granting him *priority* over all our incoming wealth. It means sacrificing a portion of that wealth to God's purposes through some system so trustworthy and reliable that we are certain he will always get a portion of current income. This includes arranging and monitoring the budget so finances are always available, and establishing a process by which we can always be reminded to give. Honoring God with our wealth means that when we are enriched, God is first in our thoughts and holds first priority in our financial allocations.

Give as a Matter of Sacrifice

The concept of firstfruits also includes the idea of sacrifice. When the ancient Israelite gave to God the best of the crop or the finest of the herd, as already noted, the experience was partly one of loss. If in giving to the Lord I am not aware of some sense of material loss—if the amount of my giving is so small as to be entirely convenient and comfortable—where is the sacrifice? Once, when David was planning to offer animals to God and another man wanted to supply the animals himself, David replied, "I will not sacrifice to the LORD my God burnt offerings that cost me nothing" (2 Samuel 24:24). If the check I write to God is for an amount that I won't even notice is missing, it might as well have been paid for me by someone else.

In other words, my giving to God should cost me something, and not merely in the literal, mathematical sense. Otherwise, while my giving may qualify as obedience (a good thing in itself), it will not be sacrificial. At best, it will be a mechanical act of obligation, which never constitutes true worship. This principle is illustrated in the New Testament in the account of the widow's offering.

As he looked up, Jesus saw the rich putting their gifts into the temple treasury. He also saw a poor widow put in two very small copper coins. "I tell you the truth," he said, "this poor widow has put in more than all the others. All these people gave their gifts out of their wealth; but she out of her poverty put in all she had to live on."

Luke 21:1–4

In other words, it's not about quantity. It's about sacrifice. The widow gave sacrificially because her giving was costly in light of her limited means. She gave her best. To give God our firstfruits is to give in a way that is truly and personally sacrificial.

To give sacrificially also means that individual or family expenses, however good and noble their purpose, or however closely related to the kingdom of God, simply don't qualify as offerings to God. This is because such expenses—the cost of Christian education, for example—are ultimately spent on ourselves. They may represent a wise and godly use of resources, but they are not given *to God* because the donor receives something tangible in return. Even the United States Internal Revenue Service recognizes that if a donor receives direct tangible benefits from an expense, it cannot be considered a gift. Honoring God with our firstfruits means giving our offering completely to him.

Give Also To the Poor

As we saw in chapter 3, the book of Proverbs strongly condemns those who become poor through their own sin. But

Proverbs also recognizes that poverty can result from injustice (13:23), oppression (14:31, 22:7, 22:16, 28:3, 29:13), or exploitation (22:22). Those who are poor due to circumstances beyond their control receive from Scripture not condemnation but compassion, and our attitude should be the same. In fact, Proverbs specifically indicates that supporting the worthy poor is one way to honor the Lord with our wealth. "He who oppresses the poor shows contempt for their Maker, but whoever is kind to the needy *honors God*" (Proverbs 14:31, emphasis added). Being "kind to the needy" clearly implies helping them in practical ways. As James admonished the early church, "Suppose a brother or sister is without clothes and daily food. If one of you says to him, 'Go, I wish you well; keep warm and well fed,' but does nothing about his physical needs, what good is it?" (James 2:15). Meaningful support of the poor may involve giving money or, in some cases, something more immediately useful such as food, clothing, or shelter. The wise and discerning financial support of parachurch ministries can be a practical way of honoring God in this area. The best ministries to the poor not only provide material support, but are committed, whenever possible, to presenting the gospel as part of their work.

When giving to the poor, ultimately we honor the one from whom all blessings flow, and God promises to reward us for this, whether materially or otherwise. "He who is kind to the poor lends to the LORD, and he will reward him for what he has done" (Proverbs 19:17; see also Proverbs 22:9 and 28:7). As we "lend to the Lord," we may be certain he will repay us. Not surprisingly, we are also warned against disobedience in this area. "If a man shuts his ears to the cry of the poor, he too will cry out and not be answered" (Proverbs 21:13; see also Proverbs 17:5).

Giving to God—first to the church but also to the poor—is not merely a command, duty, and obligation, but also a privilege and a joy. To give to the worthy poor is an important way by which we honor God with our wealth.

Steward God's Reward

> Honor the LORD with your wealth, with the firstfruits of all your crops; then your barns will be filled to overflowing, and your vats will brim over with new wine.
>
> Proverbs 3:9–10

God commands us to give of our wealth regularly and faithfully, but not so that we might become poor. Rather, he requires us to give, in large part, to help us fend off idolatry and battle selfishness. And if that was the only purpose of our giving, it would be enough. But in fact, when we give biblically, we set in motion a chain of events God intends to continue. Proverbs 3:10, above, contains just one of several assurances in Scripture that when we do give biblically, God will reward us materially. The imagery is powerful: Faithfully honoring God with our wealth results in our economic storehouses being filled to overflowing, even brimming over. This can begin a cycle that increasingly redounds to God's glory.

But we must remember that above all, God wants us to "Keep [our] lives free from the love of money and be content with what [we] have" (Hebrews 13:5). Therefore, we must see God's promise of reward as a promise of *blessing* and *provision* for the purpose of *stewardship*, not *riches* for the purpose of *self-indulgence*. When God rewards us financially for biblical giving, he does so that we might learn to respond wisely, like the faithful servant in the parable of the Ten Minas from Luke 19.

Are Christians in America honoring God with their wealth? The Barna Group, a Christian research firm, reported that in 2007:[17]

101

- The percentage of born-again adults who gave any money to churches dropped to its lowest level this decade (76%).
- ... money donated by born-agains to churches as a proportion of all of the money born-agains gave away has also dropped precipitously.[18]

This can only mean that a great many Christians in the United States are not being materially rewarded by God because they are not honoring him with their wealth. Although a portion of God's rewards will only be realized in the age to come, the promise always holds: Those who honor God with their wealth will be enriched by him. Let us be sobered, then, by the two-sided nature of Paul's admonition in 2 Corinthians 9:6–7: "Remember this: Whoever sows sparingly will also reap sparingly, and whoever sows generously will also reap generously." And certainly let us not be as the Israelites who refused to give to God from their wealth and as a result suffered this judgment and rebuke: "You earn wages, only to put them in a purse with holes in it" (Haggai 1:6).

Thus, another way to honor God with our wealth is to steward wisely what he gives to us. If we fail to honor the Lord with our wealth, we will not receive from God the greater wealth he wants to give us. But if we do so honor him, he will pour out more. His purpose in this is that we might, in turn, become even better stewards of wealth, increasingly honoring God with our finances and bringing him ever more glory.

Live According to Your Means

> One man pretends to be rich, yet has nothing; another pretends to be poor, yet has great wealth.
>
> Proverbs 13:7

We also honor God with our wealth when we live according to our means, rather than pretending we are substantially richer or poorer than we really are. The Bible is never easy on pretenders, for when pretending amounts to a denial of reality, it is a form of lying. This is offensive to God because this world he has created is one of true, objective realities, and he expects us to live honestly within those realities, as best we can perceive them. Certainly, if we are to honor God with our wealth, we must begin by acknowledging the extent of our wealth, whether much or little. Proverbs 13:7, above, identifies two categories of financial pretenders: the poor who pretend to be rich, and the rich who pretend to be poor.

Don't Pretend To Be Rich

The person who pretends to be wealthier than he really is craves respect, attention, and/or self-indulgence. He is more concerned with pleasing himself by portraying a fantasy than he is with pleasing God by living in reality. Often he is also an idolater, convinced that the key to satisfaction is found in the things that money can buy, or in having a reputation for being prosperous.

The materialist culture constantly tells us that we have a right to surround ourselves with all manner of comforts and conveniences. The financial system tells us that, thanks to easy credit, each of us can have whatever we want, without waiting. At the end of the year 2000, the average household in the United States carried a credit card balance of approximately $10,000.[19] So many of us, Christian and non-Christian alike, are enslaved to indebtedness. Apparently we believe that the most important thing is to live as if we are rich, even if we aren't. All the while, we hang onto the notion that surely happiness is right around the corner . . . just one more gadget, one more piece of clothing, one more vacation.

Don't Pretend To Be Poor

The person who pretends to be less wealthy than he really is has a different sort of problem. Certainly, Proverbs 13:7 is not intended to encourage the rich to flaunt their wealth and live ostentatiously. Rather, the wealthy can pretend to be poor in a selective sort of way. We may have plenty of money for ourselves, but surprisingly little to give to the church or the truly poor. If so, we are simply refusing to take full responsibility for what God has given us. To some degree we reject the greater stewardship role to which we have been called. Our practice of stewardship has not grown along with our bank account. In that sense, we live in denial of the increased responsibilities and obligations that come with increased wealth. We live as if we were poor.

This is illustrated dramatically in the book of Haggai, which describes the effort to rebuild the temple of God that had been destroyed by the Babylonians. When it comes time to collect an offering to fund the project, the wealthy, self-indulgent Israelites pretend to be poor, and suffer a rebuke from God as a result. Here what God says through Haggai:

> This is what the LORD Almighty says: "These people say, 'The time has not yet come for the LORD's house to be built.'" Then the word of the LORD came through the prophet Haggai: "Is it a time for you yourselves to be living in your paneled houses, while this house remains a ruin?"
>
> Haggai 1:2–4

The Israelites had returned from captivity back to Jerusalem and gradually became wealthy. As riches accumulated, they found it easy to spend some extra money on themselves. But when asked to give some of it away—to honor the Lord with their wealth—suddenly they felt poor.

Don't Do Both at the Same Time

In terms of our temptations, you and I are no different from the Israelites. When it comes to honoring *ourselves* with our wealth, our tendency is to think and act as if we are richer than

104

we really are. But when it comes to honoring God with our wealth, our tendency is to think and act as if we are poorer! We try to appear rich toward our fellow men, then we have the unholy boldness to tell God we can't afford to honor him financially. What a testimony to our selfishness! In the first instance, we are discontent with our riches, in effect blaming God for not giving us more. As a result, we tend to get ourselves into debt, crippling our ability to honor God with our wealth, even if we wanted to. In the second instance, we "rob God" (Malachi 3:8), neglecting the one who has given us "life and breath and everything else" (Acts 17:25).

Let us not foolishly pretend to be something we are not. Let us live according to our means, truly honoring God with whatever degree of wealth he has given us.

Leave an Inheritance

A good man leaves an inheritance for his children's children, but a sinner's wealth is stored up for the righteous.

Proverbs 13:22

We have learned that the Bible teaches us to diligently acquire wealth, and even commends those who acquire more than they absolutely need. We are commanded then to honor the Lord with our wealth, because (just like everything else we might think we own) it really isn't ours; we have only received it as a gift from God. A prayer of the psalmist David recorded in 1 Chronicles 29 includes, "Who am I, and who are my people, that we should be able to give as generously as this? Everything comes from you, and we have given you only what comes from your hand."

So far in this chapter we have seen that we can honor the Lord with our wealth by giving financially to God and his work, by helping the innocent poor, by stewarding well what we have received, and by living honestly in light of whatever wealth we have been given. Finally, we can honor God with our wealth by leaving an inheritance.

Proverbs 13:22, above, gives us a glimpse of what tends to happen to wealth in this world, a world that exists under the authority of God's all-encompassing laws. When those who truly honor God with their wealth die, they tend to leave behind a financial sum large enough to have an effect on more than one generation of heirs. The wealth of those who honor God tends to persist, accumulate, and be passed along to subsequent generations. But for those who do not honor God with their wealth, what riches they do accumulate tend to be transferred to the righteous.

Notice how the first part of Proverbs 13:22 focuses on specific actions taken by those who please God: "A good man *leaves* . . ." In the second part, however, the emphasis is on something more passive—what *happens to* the wealth of the sinner, completely outside of his control, after he has stored it away: "A sinner's wealth is *stored up for* the righteous." Where our money ends up will depend on how we use it. If we use it in ways that honor God, it will tend to persist, accumulate, and be passed to our children. If we do not, it will tend to flow to those who *will* use it as God intends. Thus, this verse pulls back the curtain and gives us a glimpse of the underlying spiritual dynamics of God's economic laws, from which ultimately there is no escape.

In addition to revealing an underlying economic reality, this verse also functions as a command to us as believers by portraying for us the actions of an ideal believer. A "good man" does something very specific. He seeks to think about, acquire, and use wealth biblically, with an eye toward amassing enough to have an impact on future generations. He endeavors to grow and preserve his wealth, not only for his children, but for his children's children. Because there was no way in the ancient world to create a trust fund for your grandchildren, the idea here involves both passing down riches and leading by example.

As we leave a financial inheritance for our children and teach them to honor God with wealth, they will themselves amass more wealth and in turn leave *their* children an inheritance. In contrast, the sinner's wealth is ultimately transferred to the righteous. Solomon speaks of this dynamic in Ecclesiastes 2:26, "To the sinner [God] gives the task of gathering and storing up wealth to hand it over to the one who pleases God." This basic spiritual principle runs throughout the entire Bible: The godly receive an inheritance while the ungodly are dispossessed.

When the Hebrews were led by Moses out of Egypt, they carried away with them vast riches, freely given over by their Egyptian masters. "The LORD had made the Egyptians favorably disposed toward the people, and they gave them what they asked for; so they plundered the Egyptians" (Exodus 12:36). When the people later entered the Promised Land, God gave them the accumulated wealth of many heathen Canaanite tribes. And in an ultimate and infinitely superior manifestation of this dynamic, upon the Lord's return an entire new creation will become the exclusive domain of those who have been counted righteous in Christ.

As with any other material blessing, the purpose of providing a financial inheritance to our heirs is not so that they might become self-indulgent. Rather, it is so they might be more useful to the work of God in the earth than we have been. If we have passed on to our children a spiritual inheritance as well as a financial one, they are likely to be better equipped than we were to resist the temptations of riches, and thus better able to put their wealth to work for God.

For example, a financial inheritance may help people live debt-free. This liberates them to give more generously to the church and the poor. Substantial inheritances can be used to help establish charitable endowments to cure diseases, expand hospitals, or fund Christian education. A great many Christian organizations and institutions struggle to make ends meet, and quite often their gifted and dedicated employees are underpaid. Much of this could be remedied by the righteous stewarding of inherited wealth to the glory of God.

On the level of the individual family, even a relatively small financial inheritance can allow a household to be supported on one income, so that mothers do not have to work outside the home during the childrearing years. Such an inheritance may also help fund a better education for children. Leaving an inheritance to our children creates a legacy which cannot be measured in merely financial terms.

Regardless of whether we can leave our children a large financial inheritance, all Christians are able to leave a spiritual legacy to their children. Indeed, the ultimate and most important inheritance we leave is not our money, but our faithful example of service to the kingdom of God. As we leave a spiritual inheritance, even if we cannot leave a significant financial one, we position our children to take up where we have left off and build a legacy both spiritual and financial. As they honor God with their wealth, our children will then receive more from him, and the cycle of slow but ever-expanding growth for the glory of God and the funding of his works can continue. Truly, the most valuable inheritance we can pass to our children is spiritual in nature.

So, if we wish to live wisely in light of the economic realities God has established, we will think about, acquire, and use wealth biblically, with an eye toward amassing enough to have an impact on future generations. To do this, we will grant God priority over all our incoming wealth. We will give to the local church in a way that is genuinely sacrificial. We will support the worthy poor. We will see God's promise of reward for giving to him as a promise of *blessing* and *provision* for the purpose of *stewardship*, not *riches* for the purpose of *self-indulgence*. We will live according to our means, rather than pretending we are substantially richer or poorer than we really are. And we will leave our children an inheritance that may well be financial, but is primarily and most importantly spiritual.

As Charles Bridges wrote, "And if there is no earthly substance to leave; yet a church in the house; a family altar; the record of holy example and instruction; and above all, a store of believing prayer laid up for accomplishment, when we shall be silent in the grave—will be an inheritance to our children of inestimable value."[20]

PART FOUR

Friends

A Proverbs-Driven Life knows
that friendship is intended
to be redemptive.

7

Like Sam to Frodo

The Redemptive Power of Godly Friendship

A man of many companions may come to ruin, but there is a friend who sticks closer than a brother.

Proverbs 18:24

---

*O*ne of my favorite pieces of literature is the *Lord of the Rings* trilogy; J.R.R. Tolkien's classic tale in which a friendship between two Hobbits succeeds in destroying the evil Ring of Power and liberating Middle Earth. Strong friendships are seen everywhere in these books: Gandalf and Bilbo, Merry and Pippin, and Legolas and Aragorn among them. Yet a central feature of the entire epic is the extraordinary bond between Frodo and Sam. In the hands of a master like Tolkien, such otherworldly fantasy can speak volumes about this world's reality, and from his Hobbits we learn rich, practical, and very human lessons about true friendship.

Here, as the two Hobbits are leaving the Shire on their grim mission to destroy the ring, Frodo says:

"It is going to be very dangerous, Sam. It is already dangerous. Most likely neither of us will come back."

"If you don't come back sir, then I shan't, that's certain," said Sam. "'Don't you leave him!' they said to me. 'Leave him!' I said. 'I never mean to. I am going with him, if he climbs to the Moon, and if any of those Black Riders try to stop him, they'll have Sam Gamgee to reckon with,' I said."[21]

Out of the boldness and depth of their friendship, Sam then accompanies Frodo on their grueling journey. Through two books of trials and dangers, Sam never wavers, continually bolstering Frodo in spirit. And at the end, as Frodo's strength fails him, Sam literally carries Frodo on his back up the side of Mount Doom, where at last the ring can be destroyed, and Middle Earth redeemed.

The Road to Redemption

You've probably never made your way across a trackless waste, loyal friend by your side, on a desperate quest to save a world from the grip of moral and spiritual darkness. But you don't need that ultimate bonding experience to know the value of friendship. Indeed, deep friendship is universally treasured as one of the best things in life. And no wonder: The desire for it is woven into our very nature, for we are made in the image of the triune God who is himself the ideal society. We are built for the experience of deep, lasting friendship, and few things are more rewarding in this life.

Among Christians, friendship has the unique potential to be redemptive as well as rewarding. The gospel of Christ's life, death, and resurrection is about God being glorified in all things as all things are becoming redeemed through him. Redemption can therefore take place at every level and in every moment. Any act or decision that furthers God's purpose is redemptive.

Jesus certainly understood well the redemptive power of friendship. For example, when he sent out his disciples to reap the harvest, he sent them out "two by two" (Luke 10:1). That is, he sent them as friends. Couldn't the disciples have covered double the ground if Jesus had sent them out individually? Yes, but obviously not with the same effectiveness. He sent them in pairs because he understood that friendship enables us to do extraordinary things; things we would not be able to do on our own. This is because the Christian life is inescapably corporate. We need each other. "Two are better than one, because they have a good reward for their toil. For if they fall, one will lift up his fellow. But woe to him who is alone when he falls and has not another to lift him up!"(Ecclesiastes 4:9–10). A Proverbs-driven life is most ably lived in the company of godly friends.

Such friends, however, can be hard to gain and all too easy to lose. We so readily sin against one another, take offense where none was intended, or permit neglect to creep in. Left to ourselves, it can be difficult to know what words and deeds will strengthen and maintain our most vital relationships. How does it all work? What are the elements of broad, deep, redemptive friendship? What can get us beyond the kind of relationship that's based on little more than, "Hey, we both like sports!" (or books or technology or the arts or cooking or theology . . .)?

In this chapter, we will examine some key verses in Proverbs to learn about a level of friendship that Jesus alone makes possible. When pursued and practiced with biblical wisdom, friendship among Christians can be richly, consistently redemptive. It is this kind of friendship for which each of us deeply yearns, and in which God delights.

Three Marks of Redemptive Friendship

When Proverbs speaks of friendship, the reference is to non-romantic relationships, generally same-sex friendships. As wonderful as marriage can be, men need male friends and women need female friends. It's just that simple. C.S. Lewis, a man who knew the satisfactions of deep romantic love, noted that one of his greatest joys came through his relationships with male friends, "My happiest hours are spent sitting up to the small hours in someone's college room talking nonsense, poetry, theology, metaphysics over beer, tea and pipes. There's no sound I like better than adult male laughter."[22]

The book of Proverbs identifies at least three factors that are central to redemptive friendships: counsel, correction, and comfort. We will examine these three by focusing on a single proverb each.

A Friend Gives Earnest Counsel

Perfume and incense bring joy to the heart,
and the pleasantness of one's friend springs from his
earnest counsel.

Proverbs 27:9

Throughout our lives we are faced with many major decisions: where to go to college, whom to marry, where to work. Is it time to change jobs? How should we discipline and educate our children? Should we buy a house? Where should we invest our money? What church should we attend? Besides these, life regularly presents us with lesser yet still significant decisions.

As Proverbs 15:22 tells us, "Plans fail for lack of counsel, but with many advisers they succeed." Do you want more of your plans to succeed? More of your decisions to be good and wise? Proverbs 27:9 advises you to seek "earnest counsel." This is selfless, sincere guidance that has the friend's best interests at heart. Neither trite nor offered in haste, it is thoughtful, wise, godly counsel, always in keeping with Scripture, and shared after appropriate reflection and expressed with genuine concern. Such counsel is so rare and valuable that the writer compares it to perfume and incense, some of the most precious and delightful treasures of the ancient world.

Notice that this verse is not saying that the best part of true friendship is how we mirror ourselves back to one another in a mutual admiration society. Rather, earnest counsel points out where we may be thinking wrongly in regard to a pending issue, circumstance, or decision. It introduces factors we had not considered, or had not considered seriously enough. Earnest counsel may at first be difficult to hear. But when wisely given and humbly received, we discover with joy that it is one of the elements that makes redemptive friendship so pleasant. Some translations of Proverbs 27:9 render "pleasant" as "sweet," for truly such earnest counsel is the "sweet spot" of biblical friendship.

A Friend Gives Trustworthy Correction

Wounds from a friend can be trusted, but an enemy multiplies kisses.

Proverbs 27:6

Correction is similar to counsel, for each one involves speaking the truth in love (Ephesians 4:15). Yet the difference between them is an important one, and helpful to understand. As we have seen, counsel generally helps keep us from heading down the wrong path in some particular area. But correction becomes necessary when we are already on the wrong path and need to change. In other words, where typically the goal of counsel is to prevent something bad, the goal of correction is to restore something good.

Proverbs 27:6 contrasts how true friends and enemies (posing as friends) respond to us when we are in the wrong. With brevity and brilliance, this verse uncovers both the worldviews and the motivations of the two groups.

The true friend is able to look at our lives with a biblical, God-centered worldview. If we are on a wrong path, he or she is able to see that as the simple, unambiguous reality that it is—no fudging about sin and deception, no flirtation with compromise. At that point, redemptive friendship can only respond one way. Wounds, in the form of verbal correction or even rebuke, have simply become necessary. There is no point in pretending the situation is not serious. Like setting a broken bone or performing surgery to remove a cancer, a friend's wounds are far better suffered sooner rather than later. These are careful, measured wounds, humbly administered, which can help heal a significant illness. Such wounding is an act of redemptive love.

An enemy, operating from a false, man-centered worldview, can only misrepresent the nature of the path we are on. Instead of corrections, there are kisses—seductive congratulations and flattering compliments that dull our vision and draw us further down the false path. These are curses masquerading as blessings. Denying reality, they do nothing but delay the pain of reality, which will be all the worse and all the more damaging when it finally and inevitably arrives.

Charles Bridges artfully illuminates the nature of a true friend:

What is the friend, who will be a real blessing to my soul? Is it enough, that he will humour my fancies, and flatter my vanity? Is it enough that he loves my person, and would spend his time and energies in my service? This comes far short of my requirement. I am a poor straying sinner, with a wayward will and a blinded heart; going wrong at every step. The friend for my case is one, who will watch over me with open rebuke; but a reprover when needful; not a flatterer. The genuineness of a friendship without this mark is more than doubtful; its usefulness utterly paralyzed.[23]

A Friend Gives Consistent Comfort

A friend loves at all times, and a brother is born for adversity.
Proverbs 17:17

Counsel and correction are applied in specific circumstances. When I am trying to choose a path, a true friend offers sound counsel. When I am on the wrong path, a true friend offers loving correction. But Proverbs 17:17 tells us what such a friend does under all circumstances, and especially when life gets hard. At all times, even in adversity, a friend offers comfort ("love"). In the original Hebrew, the phrase "at all times" is placed at the beginning of this proverb, emphasizing its centrality.

Proverbs 17:17 therefore gives us a way of discerning whether our friendships are truly "brotherly." Those who continue to offer comfort faithfully during seasons of adversity are friends in the truest, most biblical sense. William Arnot explains the power of adversity in identifying a true friend:

> Many will court you while you have much to give; when you need to receive, the number of your friends will be diminished, but their quality will be improved. Your misfortune, like a blast of wind upon the thrashed corn, will drive the chaff away, but the wheat will remain where it was. How very sweet sometimes is the human friendship that remains when sore adversity has sifted it![24]

Those who, despite the harsh winds of adversity, faithfully remain by your side to offer comfort are true friends, for they "bear one another's burdens, and so fulfill the law of Christ" (Galatians 6:2).

Jonathan was such a friend to David. Young David, anointed by God to be King over Israel, posed a threat to the enthroned monarch, the increasingly unstable King Saul. Saul's arrogance before God had disqualified him from reigning, yet he clung to his position, hating and fearing the favor of God resting on David. So for many years, Saul relentlessly pursued David, seeking to kill him.

On many occasions during this season, David felt he did not have a friend in the world and that his entire life was collapsing around him. But in the midst of this severe adversity, God supplied David with the friendship of Jonathan. So committed was Jonathan to David that he had pledged a friendship covenant ("And Jonathan made a covenant with David because he loved him as himself," 1 Samuel 18:3), a covenant Jonathan kept despite being the son of King Saul. Jonathan could have rested in his place of royal privilege, but he chose to help David bear the burden of mortal peril. What risks Jonathan took to remain loyal to a man his own father sought to kill! What comfort that loyalty gave David in his days of distress!

In our day, biblical comfort can be both tangible and intangible. But in one way or another, such comfort always demonstrates and underscores the truth of the gospel. Having been purchased for God through the sacrifice of the Son, we are eternally secure. God has nothing but unending love for us. Whatever the circumstances, we have the reality of sins forgiven and righteousness bestowed. In this truth we find a comfort that can transcend all the trials and adversities of life.

The pursuit and practice of counsel, correction, and comfort are indispensable to the creation and maintenance of redemptive friendships, and they are markers of relationships characterized by biblical wisdom.

Giving and Receiving

Before concluding this chapter I want to mention one additional verse from Proverbs that helps us see how friendship can be redemptive. Proverbs 27:17 offers this well-known metaphor, "As iron sharpens iron, so one man sharpens another." The writer was probably thinking of one of these pieces of iron as a sword or knife, and the other as a sharpening stone. An effective cutting edge, of course, is not sharpened by constant coddling, but by the periodic, skillful application of constructive, appropriate force. This verse presents a vivid image of a blade (one person) being sharpened by the force of direct contact with a sharpening stone (another person). Such sharpening can take many forms. Where the "blade" of one's life is dull and pitted, the sharpening of a friend may feel like strong correction. See how Nathan corrected David in 2 Samuel 12:1–15. At these times, we will do well to remember David's testimony in Psalm 141:5, "Let a righteous man strike me—it is a kindness; let him rebuke me—it is oil for my head; let my head not refuse it." But where our edge is good and clean, sharpening can feel more like counsel—less firm and vigorous, yet still necessary and helpful.

Do you have a friend who offers counsel, correction, and comfort? Is there a righteous man or woman in your life who knows how to sharpen the edge of your faith? Only the proud refuse these things (as we all do sometimes), and only those who have gone on to be with Christ are beyond the need of them. So in humility, seek such friends, and let them serve you.

More importantly, be such a friend to others—because the battle against sin never ends, and the world, the flesh, and the devil continually conspire to deceive us. Here is the reality:

- There are men in your church who feel they are in dead-end jobs. Others see themselves as failed husbands and fathers. Some cannot recognize the hope they have in God, and suffer from depression. All will struggle from time to time with sexual temptation.

- There are women in your church who feel exhausted from their duties as homemakers and mothers. They feel desperately alone, starving for adult conversation and a sympathetic ear. Others are going through difficult, major adjustments. Some are moving from career track to mommy track. Some are struggling with fertility. Still others are fighting chronic illnesses and experiencing marital strife.

Your church is filled with people who are desperate for redemptive friendship. Sometimes those most in need are the ones who appear mature, balanced, and always in control. Who will be the David benefiting from your role as Jonathan, the Frodo rejoicing in your role as Sam?

And when you are the needy one, as we all are at times, will you allow another to be your brother or sister "born for adversity"? Let us not be experts at internalizing pain and deflecting offers of help, but let us be humble, acknowledging our need, and grateful to God for his provision of faithful, redemptive friendships.

Redemptive friendships remind us what our redemption truly means. In the giving and receiving of counsel, correction, and comfort, let the power of redemptive friendship characterize life in your church.

Friends of the Redeemer

Our need for redemptive human friendship is real and vitally important. Christlike friends are gifts of God's grace who remind us of Christ and point us to Christ. But as good and rich and pleasing to God as these relationships can be, they are obviously no replacement for the friendship of the One who makes it all possible.

Our greatest need is for a friendship that transcends the friendships of this world. We need the friendship of our Lord Jesus. Jesus brings us all the blessings of friendship in their highest forms. He is the friend who provides continual earnest counsel through his Word. He is the friend who rebukes and corrects us in love. He is the friend who provides us with *the* Comforter—the Holy Spirit. Jesus Christ is the friend who sticks with us at all times, promising never to leave us or forsake us (Hebrews 13:5) and promising to be with us to the very end of the age (Matthew 28:20).

Does it seem inappropriate or irreverent to you to think of Jesus as a friend? If so, recall that it was he who first applied the term "friend" to his relationship with his disciples:

My command is this: Love each other as I have loved you. Greater love has no one than this, that he lay down his life for his friends. You are my *friends* if you do what I command. I no longer call you servants, because a servant does not know his master's business. Instead, I have called you *friends*, for everything that I learned from my Father I have made known to you.

John 15:12–15, emphasis mine

Jesus is our best, greatest, surest, wisest, most faithful friend. Our earthly friendships reflect only the smallest fraction of the glory of his heavenly and divine friendship.

At the start of this chapter appears Proverbs 18:24, "A man of many companions may come to ruin, but there is a friend who sticks closer than a brother." This friend is ultimately Jesus Christ, for all human friendships are actually secondary, derived from God's friendship toward his people. It is the friendship of the Son toward those for whom he died that is primary, essential, and definitive. Cultivating our friendship with him is the wisest and most redemptive of all actions.

8

Lot's Decline and Ruth's Example

Reaching out in Wisdom

He who walks with the wise grows wise, but a companion of fools suffers harm.

Proverbs 13:20

There is a moment in *The Lord of the Rings* when the reader (or movie watcher) gets an allegorical glimpse of what can happen to the gentlest of souls when it keeps company with evil long enough. The scene takes place as the Hobbits, Frodo and Sam, arrive at Rivendell, home of the Elves. After arriving at the magnificent grounds, Frodo becomes reunited with his kindly uncle Bilbo, who had secretly owned the evil ring for many years. Bilbo knows Frodo is on a mission to take the ring to Mount Doom to destroy it, and at one point he catches sight of it dangling from a chain around Frodo's neck. Suddenly, and just for a moment, this gentle uncle is horribly transformed. In the movie version, as Bilbo lunges for the ring, we see his face bloom in an instant into that of a furious, lusting demon that bears only the slightest resemblance to the elderly Hobbit. The moment passes quickly, leaving everyone, Bilbo most of all, shocked, embarrassed, and appalled at this grotesque manifestation of the ring's evil work.

Tolkien wanted his books to reflect central themes of Scripture, prominent among them the fact that evil is seductive, and exposure to it can harm us. Proverbs 13:20, our focus for this chapter, tells us plainly that we become like those with whom we spend time; growing either more wise and good or more foolish and wicked. In the previous chapter, we saw how godly friendships help us to be more like Christ. Now we want to examine the dangers of foolish friendships, defined in Scripture as those that bring us in close contact with evil.

Proverbs has much to say regarding the dangers of foolish companionships, but its teaching on the subject can be summarized as involving two processes. Unwise associations can lead us to become *disarmed* and then *destroyed*. We'll look at both of those in this chapter, but first there is a question we must deal with.

Should I Ever Be Friends With An Unbeliever?

Although Proverbs warns repeatedly against associating with the morally corrupt, this does not mean a Christian can never have non-Christian friends. Remember, Proverbs is not a book of laws, but a book of wisdom. The warnings there are not requirements. Rather, the wisdom books of Scripture are intended to inform us, to give us tools by which we can make good, godly decisions.

Elsewhere, of course, Scripture encourages and even commands us to associate with unbelievers. In the New Testament, the church is called to go to all nations and disciple them for Christ (Matthew 28:19). This institutionalizes in the church a constant outward focus, a permanent emphasis on reaching out to non-Christians. Our Savior himself was notorious for associating with the worst sorts of sinners (Luke 15:2), even eating with prostitutes and tax collectors, the lowest of the low in that society. It was plain to all that Jesus made a habit of regularly spending time with "the wrong crowd." Clearly, there are many times when the most godly thing we can do is interact with those most in need of the gospel.

So, numerous proverbs warn us against unwise associations. Yet it's plain that some associations with unbelievers, and even with hardened sinners, aren't unwise at all, but necessary to living out our faith! How do we know, then, when it's wise to associate with a non-Christian?

As much as we might like to have a simple answer to that question, there isn't one. Each situation must be judged on its own merits. But let me offer a guiding principle that can often help bring a measure of clarity to a particular situation. It may be best stated as a question: "Is this friendship or association drawing the unbeliever to God, or is it drawing me away from God?" Stated another way: "Is this friendship or association leading the unbeliever to the light, or is it drawing me to the darkness?" Let's look at one biblical example of each dynamic.

Leading to the Light: The Friendship of Ruth and Naomi

The story of Ruth and Naomi, recorded in the book of Ruth, begins with a series of tragic events. First, Israel suffers a famine which forces Naomi, her husband, and her two sons to move to the pagan region of Moab in order to find food. Naomi's husband dies, and some time later Naomi's two sons marry Moabite women, Orpah and Ruth. When Naomi's sons die as well, Orpah and Ruth choose to live with Naomi.

So here is Naomi, her husband and sons dead, living in a heathen land with her sons' Gentile widows. Having heard that the famine in Israel was over, Naomi decides to return to Israel. Orpah and Ruth begin to travel with her, but shortly after the journey begins, Naomi counsels the two young women to return to Moab. Despite having lived some ten years or more among the Moabites, Naomi's words reveal her steadfast focus on the Lord: "May the LORD deal kindly with you . . . The LORD grant that you may find rest" (Ruth 1:8–9). Orpah agrees to return to Moab, but Ruth pleads to stay with Naomi.

"Look," said Naomi, "your sister-in-law is going back to her people and her gods. Go back with her." But Ruth replied, "Don't urge me to leave you or to turn back from you. Where you go I will go, and where you stay I will stay. Your people will be my people and your God my God. Where you die I will die, and there I will be buried. May the LORD deal with me, be it ever so severely, if anything but death separates you and me."

Ruth 1:15–17

In these extraordinary verses, Ruth professes some level of faith in God and offers Naomi a pledge of unending friendship. Naomi responds by allowing Ruth to come to Israel. Clearly, the two women have become more than traveling companions. They are now friends. As the story continues, we see the two women helping each other in many ways. While in Israel, Ruth helps to ensure Naomi's welfare by gathering food for her, and Naomi aids Ruth by helping her to find a husband.

Naomi's friendship with the unbelieving Ruth was a wise association. It was wise because it was focused on leading Ruth to God. Had it looked at any point as though Ruth was drawing Naomi into evil, then Naomi would have been best to seriously reconsider the relationship. But the dynamic was in the opposite, godly direction: Through Naomi's friendship, Ruth left Moab and its idols and embraced the true and living God.

God intends for redemptively focused friendships to be a common part of the Christian life. In fact, such a friendship was key to my own conversion. While a junior in college, I was sitting in a political philosophy class in which we were discussing the thought of the Protestant Reformer, John Calvin. I was an unbeliever at the time and considered Calvin's theology to be a bit loony. I simply could not understand how any intelligent person could believe such apparent nonsense. After class I struck up a conversation with a classmate and was utterly shocked to learn that she actually believed in Calvin's teaching! When she invited me to a meeting at her church, I took her up on it out of sheer curiosity. That church is where I first heard the gospel. Eventually, I repented of my sins and confessed Jesus Christ as my Lord and Savior. Like Ruth, I had journeyed to Israel in the company of a friend and eventually became part of that people. Also, like Ruth, I eventually married a godly spouse—the very classmate who was willing to associate with an unbeliever like me!

This is no wholesale endorsement of "missionary dating." The question posed above must always be carefully considered: "Is this friendship or association leading the unbeliever to the light, or is it drawing me to the darkness?" Any association which tends to lead an unbeliever to the light, to the church, and to the living God, is a worthy and wise one.

Drawn to the Darkness: The Association of Lot and Sodom

Of course, not all associations with unbelievers yield a positive result. The Bible provides us with a stark example of this in Lot's association with the people of Sodom.

For much of his life, Lot wisely dwelled with his uncle Abram. However, in Genesis 13, we learn that because of Abram and Lot's vast herds and many tents, the land could no longer support both of them. When the herdsmen began bickering over grazing land, Abram offered a solution to the conflict.

> So Abram said to Lot, "Let's not have any quarreling between you and me, or between your herdsmen and mine, for we are brothers. Is not the whole land before you? Let's part company. If you go to the left, I'll go to the right; if you go to the right, I'll go to the left." Lot looked up and saw that the whole plain of the Jordan was well watered, like the garden of the LORD, like the land of Egypt, toward Zoar. (This was before the LORD destroyed Sodom and Gomorrah.) So Lot chose for himself the whole plain of the Jordan and set out toward the east. The two men parted company: Abram lived in the land of Canaan, while Lot lived among the cities of the plain and pitched his tents near Sodom.
>
> Genesis 13:8–12

Lot was Abram's nephew. Surely he knew of God's dealings with Abram, in particular that Canaan was the Promised Land. But here Lot chooses to live outside of Canaan, and near the wicked city of Sodom, simply because it looks appealing. So while Abram went to live in Canaan, Lot separated himself from the covenant people and the Promised Land, and associated himself with Sodom. In New Testament terms, Lot chose the world instead of the church. This was a profoundly unwise decision.

In the land of Sodom, Lot quickly lost sight of what he knew was right. Iain Duguid traces Lot's tragic progression:

> Lot started out living '*near* Sodom' (13:12). Soon he was living '*in* Sodom' (14:12). Then he was 'sitting in the gateway of the city' (19:1), which suggests that he held a position of respect among the citizens of Sodom, and his daughters were pledged to marry inhabitants of the city (19:14).[25]

Lot made a series of sinful decisions, even offering his daughters to be sexually assaulted by a gang of men (Genesis 19:8). Instead of leading Sodom to the light, Lot and presumably

129

everyone with him was drawn ever deeper into Sodom's darkness. His is a tragic, classic case of being disarmed and then destroyed by close association with sin.

First, Disarmed

Do not make friends with a hot-tempered man, do not associate with one easily angered, or you may learn his ways and get yourself ensnared.

Proverbs 22:24–25

The way sin worked to corrupt Lot is the same way it always works. The process is almost completely predictable. Gradually we allow ourselves to be disarmed and rendered defenseless. It starts when our clear view of sin becomes clouded, and our thinking about truth gets muddled. Echoes of the serpent's voice in the Garden (Genesis 3:1) begin to enter our minds: "Has God really said" that this thing we are engaged in, or are drawn to, is actually wrong? We look out over the land where Sodom lies, and all we can see is that it looks green and lush. So we move over there and start to settle in. Suppressing the initial pangs of conscience, we slowly begin, in the language of Proverbs 22:24–25, to "learn the ways" of the corrupt.

Children and young people are especially impressionable. But even in adulthood, we can readily adopt new ways by imitating others, and often without even realizing it. Have you ever noticed yourself repeating a close friend's favorite saying or unconsciously mimicking his or her body language? We can absorb the mannerisms of others like a sponge absorbs water.

Looking at it another way, notice how this proverb refers to the sinful behavior of the hot-tempered man as if it were a communicable disease. Like a virus transmitted through close contact, unwise associations assault our spiritual immune systems and can make us spiritually ill.

But the most helpful and accurate metaphor involves the armor of God as cataloged by Paul in Ephesians 6:10–17. When we pursue unwise friendships—those that draw us into the darkness of sin—it is as if, very gradually, we unbuckle the belt of truth, remove the breastplate of righteousness, put down the shield of faith, take off the helmet of salvation, and drop the sword of the Spirit.

There we stand, disarmed and spiritually helpless. Having abandoned the God-given defenses of our faith and laid ourselves open and vulnerable to attack from spiritual forces dedicated to our defeat, what happens next should come as no surprise.

Then, Destroyed

> Fear the LORD and the king, my son, and do not join with
> the rebellious,
> for those two will send sudden destruction upon them,
> and who knows what calamities they can bring?
>
> Proverbs 24:21–22

This proverb warns against unwise associations with a particular sort of person: the one who rebels against appropriate authority, whether God or the civil authorities. It may seem at first as though this limits the scope of the proverb. But in reality, every unwise association will be with someone who rebels against authority. As Romans 13:1 makes perfectly clear, "Everyone must submit himself to the governing authorities, for there is no authority except that which God has established. The authorities that exist have been established by God." Unwise associations, by definition, are formed with those who rebel against appropriate authority.

This gives us a useful test, one that can help us remain objective when the attractiveness of sin threatens to cloud our judgment and disarm us. If I suspect I may be in an unwise friendship, I can ask myself, "Is this association encouraging me to rebel against authority?" If so—if I am adopting a rebellious attitude or actually rebelling against any legitimate authority—it doesn't matter if I can't feel or discern the sinfulness of it. I am in an unwise association, and I dare not trust my own judgments and emotions over the Word of God.

Finally, note the severity of the penalties in this verse: "sudden destruction . . . calamities." Join with wrongdoers, and you run the risk of serious consequences.

The Arc of Redemption

Lot's decision to leave the people of God and associate with the unbelieving Sodomites was unwise because it drew him to darkness. Moving ever deeper into Sodom, Lot effectively removed himself from God's protection and gradually embraced sin. He learned the rebellious ways of Sodom, rather than teaching them God's ways. In addition to becoming disarmed, Lot was also almost destroyed because of that association, narrowly escaping with his life when God's wrath was poured out on the city. His wife did not fare as well (Genesis 19:26).

But the line of Lot was far from over, for his descendants became the heathen people of Moab. And one day, many hundreds of years later, a Moabite widow named Ruth decided to accompany her mother-in-law, Naomi, back to Israel—back to the people of God her forbear Lot had withdrawn from so many generations earlier. There, she married an Israelite named Boaz, and bore him children. One was a son, and that son became part of the blood line of King David and eventually of the Lord Jesus Christ (see Matthew 1:5).

So we go full circle in this chapter: From the Abrahamic promise to Lot (as Abram's nephew); to Lot's withdrawal from Canaan and his corruption in Sodom; to a line of heathen descendants living near Canaan; to one of them coming out, returning to Israel, and entering the line of the Messiah. God is faithful to his promises, and is at work in each moment of individual lives in ways that fulfill his plan for the great arc of redemptive history.

In conclusion, Christians should have numerous associations outside the church. Being salt and light in society and engaging in evangelism is central to our calling in Christ. But we must think about and evaluate these associations somewhat differently than we do our associations with fellow believers—and we must do this carefully and often. As a result of our association with unbelievers, are we adopting mannerisms and habits that are themselves sinful or could lead to sin? Are we drifting toward rebellion against any legitimate authority? Are we being a moral and spiritual influence for good toward the unsaved, or in those associations are we being morally and spiritually influenced toward evil? A prolonged, careless attitude toward unwise associations can carry a high price. That price can include even sudden destruction and calamity, the work of a sovereign God who acts out of love and mercy to preserve us from the even greater harm that would come from our continued rebellion.

So this matter of reaching out to the lost is no small thing. It is central to our role as believers in Christ and servants of Christ, yet it introduces risks that could weaken our relationship with Christ. God knows those risks far better than we, yet he who purchased our lives on the cross still calls us to reach out in his name. We must never forget that we were all once enemies of God (Romans 5:10). We were offensive in his sight. However, the amazing glory of the gospel is contained in this truth, "While we were still sinners, Christ died for us," (Romans 5:8). As people who have had our eyes opened to the glorious and profound truth of salvation in Christ, we must build relationships with those who are still lost in their sin. But we must do so with biblical wisdom, mindful of the dangers.

Just as God loved us and associated with us while we were still sinners we must, by his grace, extend similar love, grace, compassion, and mercy to the unbelievers we associate with in our daily lives. As we do so, we just need to exercise some care.

PART FIVE

Marriage

A Proverbs-Driven Life embraces marriage as the most significant of relationships and guards it jealously.

9

Noble Character

The Wise Choice in a Spouse

Whoever finds me [wisdom] finds life and receives favor from the LORD.

Proverbs 8:35

---

*T*here is a chapter in the book of Proverbs that can puzzle Christian women, if not outright perplex them. It's chapter 31, of course, which closes out Proverbs by taking twenty-two verses to extol a truly remarkable woman. She does it all! She works endlessly, beginning before dawn and continuing until long after sundown (vv. 15, 18). At home, she makes her own clothes and bed coverings, oversees the entire household, and cares for her children (vv. 22, 27–28). Outside the home, she's a real-estate investor, runs a vineyard, and operates a small garment business (vv. 16, 24). She fears the Lord and is wise, noble, and trustworthy (vv. 10, 11, 26, 30). Oh, and she finds time to help the poor, too (v. 20). Women may look at this description and think, Who IS this person? How can she DO

137

all that? How can she BE all that? Often mixed with their amazement is a sense of not measuring up. If this is what a godly woman is supposed to be, what chance do I have?

Without going into an elaborate commentary on this passage, let me just note that Proverbs 31 is not a universal checklist or standard for godliness in women, something you either attain to or you don't. Rather, what we find in these verses are the kinds of things that women with godly character will *do*. These are some of the general areas they will *focus on*, seeking to live wisely by being productive, responsible stewards of their time, talents, and opportunities.

For purposes of this chapter, however, I want to emphasize the question in verse 10 that leads into this remarkable description: "A wife of noble character who can find?" Two clear points flow from this question. First, such women are not easy to find, for they are rare. Second, their core attribute can be summed up in two words: noble character.

Not every mature, godly woman will run a small business or be an excellent seamstress. That kind of specificity is not the point of Proverbs 31:10–22. But we can say with certainty that every such woman will possess *noble character*. From this we receive crucial insight into what a man should look for in a future spouse. If you want to find a woman who will make an excellent wife, seek a woman having noble character.

At this point, let us recall that when Proverbs was written, the cultural practice was for only men to choose spouses. Although women have always been able to encourage certain suitors and discourage others, in Solomon's day women never did the formal, public choosing. Therefore, only men received written warning and guidance to help them choose well.

Obviously, women can still find vital guidance in Proverbs as well as elsewhere in Scripture on selecting a husband, as will be emphasized throughout this chapter. Yet the prominence of Proverbs 31 has undoubtedly led more than one woman to wish the book was a chapter or so longer. Maybe if there were a Proverbs 32, men would have a parallel description of what it means for *them* to have noble character. But in fact, such a description of the ideal husband already exists, and it is easily as challenging as anything found in Proverbs 31.

When the apostle Paul writes, "Husbands, love your wives, just as Christ loved the church and gave himself up for her," (Ephesians 5:25), he is pointing husbands—and future husbands—to the ultimate ideal of noble character, the only perfect person, male or female, who has ever lived. To follow up on that command, men don't have half a chapter of Proverbs to consult. They have at a minimum a set of four books called Matthew, Mark, Luke, and John! For Paul calls these men to measure up to the standards of our Lord Jesus Christ, the perfect bridegroom of his spouse, the church.

So whether you are a woman seeking a future husband, or a man seeking a future wife, the same two-word summation serves as a sound, basic marker. While you can't know exactly how someone may grow and develop during the next ten, twenty, or fifty years, there is one thing to look for now that promises to be of great value in the future.

Noble character.

In Search of Noble Character

A wife of noble character is her husband's crown, but a disgraceful wife is like decay in his bones.

Proverbs 12:4

Proverbs devotes a great deal of attention to the subject of marriage, in part because God wants those seeking a spouse to have the benefit of divine wisdom as they choose. Selecting a spouse is often called the second most important decision a person can make (after "choosing" to follow Christ). Certainly there is a great deal at stake in deciding whom to marry, and not merely for the two people involved, but for their children, grandchildren, and the generations to follow.

One way Proverbs communicates what's at stake is by contrasting the personal consequences that can result from choosing a spouse wisely or foolishly. Let's look at Proverbs 12:4, above, to examine these consequences, both good and bad.

Choosing Wisely

Proverbs 12:4 begins by telling us the outcome of choosing wisely, "A wife of noble character is her husband's crown." Here, the metaphor of the "crown" implies that a good wife brings her husband blessings, both privately and publicly.

In the private realm, the woman becomes her husband's crown by being supportive of his call to be the leader in his home. A noble wife respects her husband's God-given authority in accordance with Paul's command in Ephesians 5:33, "and the wife must respect her husband." She crowns him through her Christ-like submission, "Wives, submit to your husbands as to the Lord," (Ephesians 5:22). The picture here is not of a wife oppressed into servitude to her husband, but rather one who willingly empowers the best characteristics of her husband's Christ-like leadership. She becomes like a glistening crown upon his head that declares to all who enter their home that this house is ordered according to Christ's command and example.

But the crown metaphor extends beyond the private realm. The crown is also a public symbol. A noble wife enhances the public stature of her husband. When in public, she honors her husband through her modesty and godly behavior. Like a crown upon the head of a king, she becomes for her husband his public glory and thus fulfils God's creative design—"the woman is the glory of man" (1 Corinthians 11:7).

The consequences of choosing wisely are clear. A man who chooses a noble wife finds a crown for his own head. He finds a woman who builds him up and does not tear him down. He finds aid and support in his calling to lead. He finds respect both privately and publicly.

For women, we find elsewhere in Scripture helpful counterparts to the crown metaphor, encouragements to choose a husband wisely. Husbands are called to love their wives sacrificially for their good, as Christ did for the church (Ephesians 5:25–27). Thus, a noble husband enhances the beauty of his wife—his crown—both publicly and privately, by praising her (Proverbs 31:28) and showing her respect (1 Peter 3:7).

So Christ is your model, ladies. Do you see something of him in that man who interests you? Do you see the noble character of the Savior resident in him? To the extent that it is, then by God's grace he has the potential to become a godly husband.

When the choice of a spouse is made wisely, the consequences are life-enhancing and God-honoring. Domestic tranquility and a good public reputation flow from wise choices in this area of life.

Choosing Foolishly

After giving us the promise of a wise choice, Proverbs 12:4 raises the stakes by warning us against a poor choice: "but a disgraceful wife is like decay in his bones." Here the external honor of the crown is contrasted with the awful prospect of inner decay.

In the private realm, such a wife can bring internal suffering to her husband by undermining his ability to lead the household as Christ has called him to do. Proverbs 27:15 captures well how a wife can wear down her husband through unwarranted criticism and constant bickering: "A quarrelsome wife is like a constant dripping on a rainy day." The imagery here goes beyond a nagging annoyance akin to a leaky faucet. This is more like a leaky roof, which over time threatens the entire structure of the home.[26] Indeed, a wife like this can render the home itself inhospitable, "Better to live on a corner of the roof than share a house with a quarrelsome wife" (Proverbs 21:9). A disgraceful wife brings sorrow, strife, and dishonor to her husband. She eats away at the core of his being. As William Arnot put it, "Woman is the very element of home, wherein all its relations and affections live and move; when that element is tainted, corruption spreads over all its breadth, and sinks into its core."[27] Proverbs reveals that an unwise choice of a spouse can destroy a household.

A man who chooses such a wife will experience decay in his bones in the public realm as well. A disgraceful wife may erode a husband's reputation through her public actions in a variety of ways. She may dress immodestly. Like Potiphar's wife, she may flirt with other men. Or she may openly berate her husband in public. Instead of a crown on his head, such a wife becomes a thorn in her husband's side.

Again, while this verse explicitly addresses the foolish choice of a wife by a husband, its wisdom implicitly works in the other direction as well. Clearly, men can behave wickedly toward their wives, causing internal suffering both privately and publicly. A disgraceful husband can destroy the entire structure of his home by abdicating his responsibilities to lead and provide. He who does so "has denied the faith and is worse than an unbeliever" (1 Timothy 5:8). He too can become like a leaky roof by constantly dripping mean-spirited criticism upon his wife. In the worst of cases, he can become verbally and physically abusive toward his wife. In public, such a man disgraces her through his adolescent behavior, his lack of leadership, and his refusal to put her needs before his own. Such a disgraceful husband causes great suffering to his wife. He is like decay in her bones.

The warnings to men about the consequences of a poorly chosen wife make the same general point to both genders: choose a spouse wisely or you set yourself up for needless pain. When the choice of a spouse is made foolishly, the consequences are life-draining and bring dishonor to God. All that flows from a foolish choice in this area of life is domestic strife and a floundering public reputation.

How to Choose Wisely

A crown on your head or decay in your bones—the contrast between the wise choice and the foolish could scarcely be more stark. It is certainly true that in Christ people can and do change. God is faithful to continually sanctify his children and make them more like himself. It is not unusual for converts to change markedly, shedding many of their old sinful ways and living far more godly and holy lives. Yet the warnings found in Proverbs are there for a reason. All of us have besetting sins and habitual sin patterns that tend to reemerge from time to time. The focus in Proverbs is on discerning and evaluating these tendencies, and choosing wisely in light of them. But how can we be certain we are making a wise choice?

The book of Proverbs offers no guaranteed formulas for success. Choosing a spouse is not a matter of mathematics. Marriage will always have risks because it occurs between two sinners in a fallen world. But Proverbs does offer universally helpful guidance in this area. Applying a New Testament perspective to the matter, this guidance can be distilled into three phrases: seek Christ, seek character, and seek counsel.

Seek Christ

Houses and wealth are inherited from parents, but a prudent wife is from the LORD.

Proverbs 19:14

Before we ever seek a spouse, we must first seek Christ. While sound human evaluation of a potential spouse is important, it is even more important to recognize that a good spouse is ultimately a gift from God. Making much the same point as Proverbs 19:14, above, Proverbs 18:22

says, "He who finds a wife finds what is good and receives favor from the LORD."

Given this reality, we should attend to the matter of choosing a spouse by first pursuing God, and then by pursuing God's assistance in our search. The best thing you can do, for yourself and your future mate, is to cultivate a deep relationship with Jesus before you even consider commencing a romantic relationship, for marriage will find its deepest taproot in the soil of genuine faith. When that matter of your relationship with Christ is well settled, and it seems time to consider marriage, then seek the guidance, wisdom, and blessing of God in finding and choosing a spouse. As William Arnot notes, "Our Father loves to be consulted in this great life-match for his children, and they who ask His advise will not be sent away without it."[28] Step one in choosing a spouse wisely is to seek the Lord for his wisdom and favor.

Seek Character

Charm is deceptive, and beauty is fleeting; but a woman who fears the LORD is to be praised.

Proverbs 31:30

After seeking Christ, the next step is to begin to act on your prayers in faith that God will meet you. Proverbs is very helpful in this regard because it tells us what to put at the very top of the "wish list"—not personal charm or physical attractiveness, but noble character and holy fear. But how can we tell if our prospective spouse has these traits? That's an easy one, for Proverbs makes clear that noble character manifests itself in noble actions.

First, as a general guide, both men and women can consult the more than seventy verses in Proverbs that describe the fool, a person clearly lacking in noble character. Do you want to know who *not* to marry? Anyone who regularly resembles the fool.

144

Second, as we revisit Proverbs 31, we are reminded that the noble wife brings good to her husband (31:12), works willingly, vigorously, and consistently (31:13, 15, 17, 18), provides food for her family (31:15), is financially thrifty and entrepreneurial (31:16, 24), assists the poor and the needy (31:20), and speaks with wisdom (31:26). Of course, the character of the noble husband can be seen through his actions as well. Such a man is self-sacrificing (Ephesians 5:25), respectful (1 Peter 3:7), gentle (Colossians 3:19), and able to lead (Ephesians 5:23–24). Noble character manifests itself in noble actions.

While these positive traits are certainly helpful in assessing the character of a prospective spouse, Proverbs tells us that a truly noble spouse possesses something more, a character trait superior to all others. In Proverbs 31, after listing all the noble actions of the good wife, the writer provides this capstone to his description of the ideal wife, "Many women do noble things, but you surpass them all. Charm is deceptive, and beauty is fleeting; *but a woman who fears the* LORD *is to be praised*" (Proverbs 31:29–30, emphasis mine). According to Proverbs, the "fear of the Lord" is the most noble of attributes and is to be prized above all other qualities.

Of course, such attributes are not created by marriage. They do not appear out of nowhere as a result of marriage. Rather, the man or woman who will manifest these traits abundantly *in marriage* will be one who has demonstrated them in a less mature form *before marriage.*

Whether it's a man seeking a woman, or a woman seeking a man, personal charm and physical attractiveness must not be primary. Clear evidence of noble character and a holy fear of God—that's what you should look for first.

Seek Counsel

Plans fail for lack of counsel, but with many advisers they succeed.

Proverbs 15:22

As we seek Christ and seek character, we must take one additional measure—we must seek the counsel of others. Proverbs advises us on the wisdom of seeking counsel, particularly when we are dealing with major life decisions such as marriage. This is especially important in matters of romance because it is so easy to be misled by our own infatuation. During a romantic courtship those rose-colored glasses of the heart can tinge everything we see with a pleasing but misleading hue. It can become easy to downplay or even completely ignore real flaws in our prospective mate. "Love is blind" may be an uninspired, lower order of proverb than what we find in Scripture, but it can certainly be true.

We also face the reality that our judgment can be thrown off by the influence of our own sin. Idolatry, for example, can become a genuine risk for the infatuated suitor. How many lovestruck men and women have convinced themselves that some particular person, their object of affection, simply *must* become their spouse? While there's nothing necessarily wrong with a deep, yearning love, that desire crosses over into idolatry when it eclipses the place of God in our lives, or when we become so certain that "God wants me to marry" him or her that we refuse even to consider any suggestions to the contrary.

Simply stated, we must trust Scripture more than we trust ourselves. We must believe what Scripture says *about us* more than we believe our own self-assessment. To humbly embrace our need for the counsel of others is to accept the fact that in a sense we must protect ourselves from ourselves. Thus, as soon as we begin to imagine that a particular person may be "the one," we will seek the counsel of many advisers. We will seek input from our parents, our pastor, and godly friends and mentors. We will find out what they think about the person who has caught our attention. Does this woman have the makings of a wife of noble character? Does this man have the makings of a Christlike, self-sacrificing husband? We will take their answers seriously, and bring the matter before the Lord in prayer.

And we will ask one additional question.

Am I a Wise Choice?

Thus far, this chapter has been addressed to people not yet married. It has also had primarily an external focus, as if the reader is peering through a telescope at the universe of potential spouses. However, in order to live a proverbs-driven life you must not only be careful to *choose* a good spouse. You must *become* someone worth choosing. This requires asking some tough questions.

For the married readers of this chapter, we too can serve our marriages and our spouses by asking ourselves some hard questions. So as we prepare to close this chapter, it will be helpful for all of us to exchange that telescope for a microscope and begin looking intently *at ourselves*.

For the Unmarried

Whether you are a woman looking for a noble husband, or a man seeking a noble wife, your first responsibility and priority is to take a sober look at yourself. After all, to be worthy of one who is noble, you must be noble yourself. Here are some key questions. With these you can begin a process of self-examination based on the teachings of Scripture.

- Are you a Christian?
- Do you fear the Lord?
- Are you committed to and active in a local church where the gospel is faithfully preached?
- Are you seeking to deepen your relationship with God through prayer and the reading and study of Scripture?
- Are you modest and humble in your dress and behavior?
- Are you wise in your speech?

- Do you display the ability to put others before yourself?
- Have you begun to prepare yourself spiritually for marriage?
- Women, are you prepared to give yourself in Christ-like submission to the man whom God calls to be your husband and your spiritual head?
- Men, have you equipped yourself theologically to be the spiritual leader of your home, and are you willing to love your wife sacrificially?

Do not trust your personal assessment of these questions. Take them before the Lord in prayer. Take them into your study of God's Word. Take them before your "many advisers" of Proverbs 15:22. To find the answers to these questions is to learn essential truths about yourself. And in becoming aware of those truths you position yourself to receive from God the grace to begin changing in whatever ways you may need to.

For the Married

This type of self-examination is not just for those who are looking for a spouse. It also applies to those who are already married. If you are married, you must inquire of yourself, "Am I becoming a more noble spouse?" Again, you can assess this by examining yourself in light of what the Bible calls us to be as husbands and wives.

If you are a wife, you can look at yourself in the mirror of Proverbs 31. The question is not whether you resemble this ideal wife in every detail, but whether your life and character parallel hers in meaningful ways, and whether you are continuing to grow spiritually in these areas.

- Do your daily activities increasingly demonstrate that husband, home, and children are high priorities for you?
- Have any of your recent actions and practices merited the praise of your husband?

- Can you realistically foresee a day when your children will rise up and call you blessed?

Then, let your inquiry expand to encompass the attributes of godly wives commended in Ephesians 5:22–24 and in 1 Peter 3:1–6. Sometimes spiritual growth does not come quickly, so let the general question be, "Over the course of the past year, have I become a more noble wife in these areas?"

If you are a husband, you also must look at yourself in the mirror of Ephesians 5.

- Are the priorities of the man in Ephesians 5 your priorities?
- Do you make some effort each day to love your wife sacrificially—in a way that is not your preference and is for her good?

Again, what you find in Ephesians 5 is a standard of perfection. The same is true with passages like Colossians 3:19 and 1 Peter 3:7. Look at each passage and ask, "Do I bear some meaningful resemblance to the men described?" and "Am I growing spiritually in these areas?"

In order to live the Proverbs-driven life you must not only choose wisely. You must also be a wise choice. The wisdom of Proverbs will equip you to do both, but you need something more than wisdom to become the spouse Jesus has called you to be—you need his empowering grace. Only Jesus can make us more like the Proverbs 31 wife or the Ephesians 5 husband, and as we seek to cooperate with him in this, he will certainly do it.

The Well of Hope

In the midst of writing the first draft of this chapter the phone rang. On the line was a friend I had not spoken with in more than two years. He had moved away and married, and I was immediately delighted he had called. Then I heard the tears in his voice as he shared the awful news. His wife had just told him she could see no alternative to divorce. My heart grieved for this man, and I could feel the decay in his bones. I don't know the details of this couple's situation or how each spouse's sin may have contributed, but their tragedy has underscored for me the truly vital importance of choosing a spouse wisely. Clearly, no other human choice is likely to affect the quality of your life on this earth to a similar degree. But what about those men and women who have already made their choice, and did not choose wisely? What do you say to a friend in such circumstances when he or she asks your counsel? What do you say to God and to yourself if the person who chose poorly is *you*? The details of a helpful, biblical answer will vary from one instance to another, but in each case the underlying answer lies in the character and promises of God.

One day, Jesus was speaking with a woman by a well in Samaria. You probably know the story. In the midst of their conversation he told her to go and bring her husband back with her to that spot. The woman, likely feeling the shame of her past sin and poor choices, replied, "I have no husband."

"Jesus said to her, 'You are right when you say you have no husband. The fact is, you have had five husbands, and the man you now have is not your husband. What you have just said is quite true'" (John 4:17–18).

Thus confronted with the reality of her poor choices and the sin associated with them, the woman admits that Jesus is right, not denying her sin or making excuses, but confessing to the truth. In response, Jesus tells her he is the Messiah, thus explaining a comment earlier in their conversation when he spoke of giving her living water. In effect, Jesus calls her to move into the future as a new creation, living by faith, forgiven of sin, and making better choices.

To all those who have felt the sting of a marriage gone awry, know that Jesus will respond to you as he did to the woman at the well. He will hear your confession, call you to repentance and change, and offer you afresh the living waters only he can give.

Our poor choices, whether made in sin or in ignorance, do have consequences. This woman's previous marriages were not erased from history. Neither repentance nor regret can change the past. But the Savior who died in our place, suffering for our sins, will always respond to our confession and repentance by offering the living water of himself, his Spirit, his truth, and his promises. In these—in Christ himself—we find our only true satisfaction and comfort, whatever our circumstances.

10

Drink the Water,
Flee the Fire

Marital Faithfulness

Drink water from your own cistern, running water from your
own well.

Proverbs 5:15

---

*W*illiam Bennet, an author and a former senior official
under Presidents Ronald Reagan and George H.W. Bush, once
attended a wedding in which the bride and groom vowed to
remain together, "as long as love shall last." Bennet quipped,
"I sent paper plates as my wedding gift."[29]

We live in a day when many marriage vows don't mean very
much, when prenuptial agreements set the stage for divorce
before the bridesmaids have selected their dresses, and when
pornography and casual sex, including adultery, are more
acceptable than at probably any other time in Western history.
Marriage, once almost universally regarded as a principled,

life-long commitment of emotional and physical faithfulness, is now widely seen as a temporary partnering of convenience. James Patterson and Peter Kim found that a shocking 53 percent of their interviewees agreed with the statement, "I will cheat on my spouse; after all, given the chance, he or she will do the same."[30] Their research led them to conclude, "While we still marry, we have lost faith in the institution of marriage. A third of married men and women confessed to us that they've had at least one affair."[31]

In stark contrast, the book of Proverbs makes a single, central, unambiguous point about faithfulness in marriage: Do not commit adultery. It conveys this as a matter of command and by way of appeal. Look at how the book unfolds. Proverbs chapter 1 strongly urges the reader to embrace wisdom. The remaining thirty chapters generally depict what wisdom looks like in particular situations, with the foolishness of adultery being addressed early and often. Chapter 2 implores and admonishes readers to embrace wisdom, avoidance of adultery being a major point of emphasis. Because we obviously need to hear it again, chapter 5, chapter 7, and half of chapter 6 are entirely devoted to warnings against adultery: sixty-five verses in those three chapters alone!

Listen to the language used in chapter 2. "Wisdom will save you from the ways of wicked men . . . it will save you also from the adulteress…for the upright will live in the land, and the blameless will remain in it; but the wicked will be cut off from the land, and the unfaithful will be torn from it." God's heart in this is not to threaten, but to warn us—to remind us that he is holy and that sin, even the forgiven sin of believers in Christ, can have serious consequences.

God despises the breaking of vows, especially in marriage, because all such behavior violates his perfect faithfulness. It is for our good that God commands our faithfulness in marriage. He wants the best for us. To embrace a lifestyle of sexual sin is to cut ourselves off from "the land"—the wholeness, truth, and fullness of joy that only life in God can provide. In the previous chapter, we looked at the importance of choosing a spouse wisely. But our desperate need for wisdom continues throughout marriage, so that we might live faithfully in it. So please hear this: If you are married, or ever hope to be married, let me encourage you not to skip past these pages. No doubt you have heard warnings against adultery, perhaps a great many times. But there is more to avoiding adultery than knowing it's wrong, and much more to the warnings of Proverbs than a simple command. This chapter can help give you the conviction and tools you need to live in true, heartfelt faithfulness to your spouse, for as long as you both shall live.

Drink the Water: Holy Sexual Desire

Drink water from your own cistern, running water from your own well. Should your springs overflow in the streets, your streams of water in the public squares? Let them be yours alone, never to be shared with strangers. May your fountain be blessed, and may you rejoice in the wife of your youth. A loving doe, a graceful deer—may her breasts satisfy you always, may you ever be captivated by her love.

Proverbs 5:15–19

Proverbs gives us two methods of maintaining marital fidelity. One is positive, encouraging us to do what is right. This encouragement employs the metaphor of water—water that is *channeled* and *contained*, resulting in *satisfaction*. As we will see later in this chapter, the other method is negative, discouraging us from sin by employing a metaphor of fire that becomes *uncontained*, resulting in *destruction*.

The water metaphor, seen in Proverbs 5:15–19, above, involves finding romantic and sexual satisfaction freely and exclusively in your spouse. The goal is to establish and maintain a delight in marital intimacy. If, as Charles Bridges put it, "[d]esire after forbidden enjoyments naturally springs from dissatisfaction with the blessing in possession,"[32] then we ought to do all we can to be fully satisfied in and by that very "blessing in possession." Let's look at the teaching of this passage so we might better understand and pursue faithfulness in marriage through the enjoyment of holy sexual desire.

Full Satisfaction . . .

May your fountain be **blessed**, and may you **rejoice** in the wife of your youth. A loving doe, a graceful deer—may her breasts **satisfy** you **always**, may you **ever** be captivated by her love.

Proverbs 5:18–19

Popular culture has cultivated a myth that monogamy is ultimately unsatisfying. Listen to that message long enough and you will think that having one sexual partner for life amounts to some kind of imprisonment. This lie can appeal strongly to our sin nature, yet Scripture teaches the polar opposite: In faithful marriage lies our greatest hope for true sexual fulfillment. Unlike the cultural gatekeepers, our Father and Creator actually knows what is best for us.

Do you see the picture painted by the Proverbs 5 passage above? It tells us that the way to full sexual satisfaction is within the free, open, joyful channel of the marital relationship. These verses feature rich language, describing the sexual relationship between husband and wife as "blessed" and something in which they can "rejoice . . . satisfy . . . always . . . ever." The writer is not prudish either, boldly encouraging the man to find consistent sexual satisfaction in his wife's body and consistent emotional attraction in her love, expressed physically.

155

... *Within Marriage*

Drink water from **your own** cistern, running water from **your own** well. Should your springs overflow in the streets, your streams of water in the public squares? Let them be **yours alone**, never to be shared with strangers. May **your fountain** be blessed, and may you rejoice in **the wife of your youth.** A loving doe, a graceful deer—may **her breasts** satisfy you always, may you ever be captivated by **her love.**

Proverbs 5:15–19

A second emphasis in these verses is on the exclusive, mutual possession of one another that is such a precious and essential part of marriage. Paul expresses this same sentiment in his first letter to the Corinthians: "The wife's body does not belong to her alone but also to her husband. In the same way, the husband's body does not belong to him alone but also to his wife" (1 Corinthians 7:4).

We see this emphasized repeatedly in Proverbs 5:15–19, above, with rapid-fire references to "your own cistern . . . well . . . fountain . . . wife," as well as in the phrases "her breasts" and "her love." The emphasis here is unmistakable. This proverb instructs and encourages married couples to quench their sexual thirst by means of one another, finding exclusive sexual satisfaction in God's gift of a spouse.

Then comes the appeal of verse 20, "Why be captivated, my son, by an adulteress? Why embrace the bosom of another man's wife?" In other words, why look elsewhere when God's plan for your sexual fulfillment is found in the person of your very own spouse?

So, in our lives we encounter two basic views on how to find true sexual satisfaction. The idea of adultery or multiple sexual partners is promoted by popular culture—the collective expression of a limited group of sinful, finite humans who are ultimately motivated by lust, greed, and pride. On the other hand, monogamous marriage is given to us as a gift by a holy, infinite God, who is entirely motivated by love and mercy. Which view seems better to believe and embrace?

Ever Captivated

> Do not deprive each other except by mutual consent and for a time.
>
> 1 Corinthians 7:5

As we look at these two passages—Proverbs 5 in the Old Testament and 1 Corinthians 7 in the New Testament—both of which emphasize how in sexual terms spouses belong exclusively to one another, we notice something interesting. In each case the negative point (Do *not* commit adultery!) is joined to the positive point (So *enjoy* sex within marriage!). As in Proverbs, so in Paul: Because a husband and wife have only one legitimate form of sexual fulfillment, let them make sure they employ it. If you intend to take seriously the sexual prohibition, which you must, then take seriously the sexual permission, as well.

Where Proverbs says this poetically by urging married couples to drink freely from the fountain and to ever be captivated by marital passion, Paul characteristically comes right to the point: "Do not deprive each other except by mutual consent and for a time, so that you may devote yourselves to prayer. Then come together again so that Satan will not tempt you because of your lack of self-control" (1 Corinthians 7:5).

In other words, if satisfying our thirst within the marriage relationship is how we are to maintain marital fidelity, spouses must not turn off the spigot. Husbands and wives alike must recognize their God-given responsibility to serve one another by genuinely desiring the sexual satisfaction of their spouse. Again, Charles Bridges was right when he said, "Tender, well-regulated, domestic affection is the best defense against the vagrant desires of unlawful passions."[33]

157

The free and regular enjoyment of sex is often easier in the early years of marriage. Even if we seek to maintain a strong biblical balance among our obligations, the challenges of parenthood, careers, active church membership, and the growing responsibilities of adulthood can pile up after a few years, stretching the limits of our time and energy. Yet between spouses, a commitment to the proper channeling of one another's sexual energies—a commitment watched closely and renewed regularly—is a cornerstone element of a lifelong, faithful, satisfying, God-glorifying marriage.

The first component of maintaining sexual fidelity within marriage involves a delightful command: Drink the water.

Flee the Fire: Sinful Sexual Desire

> Can a man scoop fire into his lap without his clothes being burned? Can a man walk on hot coals without his feet being scorched? So is he who sleeps with another man's wife; no one who touches her will go unpunished.
>
> Proverbs 6:27–29

As vital and absolutely necessary as it is to drink the water, in this area there is more to obeying Scripture and more to protecting spouse, marriage, and self. The use of water as a metaphor for holy sexual desire is paired in Proverbs with the use of fire as a metaphor for sinful sexual desire. We must not only drink the water. We must flee the fire; for there are three attributes of sexual temptation that combine to make it absolutely deadly to spiritual character and healthy marriages. It allures, spreads, and burns.

This Fire Allures

> For the lips of an adulteress drip honey, and her speech is smoother than oil.
>
> Proverbs 5:3

We do ourselves, our churches, and our children a great disservice when we pretend that infidelity is not alluring. We must speak honestly of the sometimes strong attraction of illicit sexual intimacy. Certainly, as we see in Proverbs 5:3, above, Scripture affirms that sexual temptation can be powerful. As a metaphor for sinful sexual desire, fire is something we can relate to. Much like fire, sexual temptation has an unusual ability to grab our attention. It may startle us at first, but soon we feel compelled to learn more, to focus more closely, to satisfy an odd curiosity, to desire a greater level of personal involvement and experience. We find ourselves pulled toward it, like a small child to a candle.

Mankind has always been fascinated with fire. In every generation, children must be told not to play with this warming, attractive, highly unusual phenomenon. In many ways it is utterly unique, just like sexuality, and of course, that uniqueness is part of the fascination.

In their foolishness, children who are not taught about fire will quickly discover it has negative, painful attributes of a severity they had never imagined. What foolish children don't know about fire, however, is the same thing foolish adults can so easily forget—or ignore—about sinful sexual temptation: It must be taken very seriously, because besides being alluring, it has two additional attributes.

It spreads, and it burns.

This Fire Spreads

Keep to a path far from her, do not go near the door of her house, lest you give your best strength to others and your years to one who is cruel.

Proverbs 5:8–9

America has largely discarded much of the sexual modesty that was once associated with Western civilization. This makes the total avoidance of sexual temptation nearly impossible. Any surface that displays images is now a candidate for the display of immodesty or indecency (if not actual pornography), for these things are no longer remarkable or out of the ordinary. In addition, the plots of books and movies, as well as the lyrics of popular songs, regularly portray sexual temptation as something to emulate, aspire to, yield to, and enjoy. Such overt public sexuality is both a symptom of sexual temptation's spread at the level of society, and a primary means by which it spreads within the hearts of individuals.

For anyone who makes the self-destructive choice to pursue such temptation, the way is indeed broad. Unlike the youth in Proverbs who had to roam the streets in order to encounter an adulteress, we can locate sources of temptation much more easily. George Scipione writes, "In the past, one had to travel to sleazy backstreets to find porn; now, it's only a click away on the computer and on the remote control of the cable/satellite TV. Easy, private, and nobody knows . . . except God."[34]

Once encountered and indulged, sexual temptation can spread through our lives like a wildfire. One thing leads to another. As conscience is defiled and each progressive step becomes easier, we go from being merely "near the door of her house," to giving our "best strength to others." This fire spreads by consuming what it touches, and grows by destroying what it envelopes.

That's what we mean when we say that something burns.

This Fire Burns

At the end of your life you will groan . . . at the brink of utter ruin.

Proverbs 5:11, 14

When Proverbs depicts the allure of marital infidelity, it does so in order to warn us that the allure is really a masquerade. Something sinister and deadly underlies the façade of the adulteress. The father in Proverbs 5, after describing that appeal, tells us that beyond the honeyed lips, "she is bitter as gall, sharp as a double-edged sword. Her feet go down to death; her steps lead straight to the grave" (Proverbs 5:4–5). The conclusion of Proverbs 7 reveals what happens to one who lingers long enough in her vicinity to see behind the mask.

[L]ike an ox going to the slaughter, like a deer stepping into a noose till an arrow pierces his liver, like a bird darting into a snare, little knowing it will cost him his life. . . . Many are the victims she has brought down; her slain are a mighty throng. Her house is a highway to the grave, leading down to the chambers of death.

Proverbs 7:22–23, 26–27

The Bible gives us numerous examples of those who were burned by the fire of sinful sexual desire. Think of Samson and Delilah, with Samson burned by the sapping of his strength and the suffering of Israel as a result of his downfall. Due to his many foreign wives, Solomon was burned by being enticed into idolatry. And following his adultery with Bathsheba, David's rule diminished greatly in glory and his family life was marred by sexual abuse, death, and personal and political betrayal.

The Art of Guarding

Above all else, guard your heart, for it is the wellspring of life.

Proverbs 4:23

As difficult as it can be to block out all exposure to sexual temptation in modern society, we must not let the pervasiveness of temptation dull us to its danger. We must walk through life consciously aware that in this fallen world are actual threats to our souls and our marriages. Therefore, we must be prepared to avoid all such temptation that we can. We must be prepared to guard our hearts.

In the tragedy of David, we find by way of negative example two behaviors that every married person must avoid. (This, and much else in this chapter, obviously applies to the unmarried as well!) We must watch where we go, and watch what we focus on—in other words: what we expose ourselves to and what we pay attention to.

Watch Where You Go

David's first error is clearly seen in the following passage. "In the spring, at the time when kings go off to war, David sent Joab out with the king's men and the whole Israelite army. . . . But David remained in Jerusalem" (2 Samuel 11:1). If it was "the time when kings go off to war," why did King David *send* Joab and *remain* in the palace? Temptation often begins when we allow ourselves to be places we ought not to be.

For us, being in the wrong place once meant almost exclusively, as we have noted, being in the wrong neighborhood, on the wrong street, or in front of the wrong house or business. Today, of course, it is much more common to be in the wrong virtual conversation, on the wrong web site, or in front of the wrong movie. In school or the workplace, one may also be spending too much time in proximity to the wrong person. Don't play games in these areas, and don't take chances. Remember that fire allures before it spreads and burns. Don't put yourself in places, virtual or actual, where you ought not to be.

Watch What You Focus On

David's second error was allowing himself to become fixated on Bathsheba. "One evening David got up from his bed and walked around on the roof of the palace. From the roof he saw a woman bathing. The woman was very beautiful, and David sent someone to find out about her. . . . Then David sent messengers to get her" (2 Samuel 11:2–4).

Clearly, David took more than a passing glance at Bathsheba. He studied her long enough to know she was beautiful, long enough to know he wanted her, and long enough to determine which house she was in so he could send someone to find her. As Philip Ryken notes, "Looking is not the problem. The problem is looking at someone in a way that leads to sexual arousal."[35] This is what David did with Bathsheba. He looked at her lustfully. Again Ryken writes, "If David had simply caught a glimpse of the woman, he would not have been guilty, but he did more than that. His glance became a gaze. He ogled the woman, looking her up and down, thinking about what he'd like to do with her."[36]

Jesus speaks to this very subject of the eyes and imagination. "You have heard that it was said, 'Do not commit adultery.' But I tell you that anyone who looks at a woman lustfully has already committed adultery with her in his heart" (Matthew 5:27–28). Men, particularly younger men, are especially prone to the kind of visual fixation Jesus speaks of here. This is one thing that makes the Internet unusually challenging and dangerous for men. If David somehow had access to the Internet, with a few clicks he could have found more illicit images than were to be seen from 100 roofs on 100 nights in Jerusalem.

While visual fixation can also be a temptation for women, most women are more prone to romantic and emotional fixation. Once again, the Internet can be a major problem; the many forms of communication made possible by the Internet can provide fertile ground for such fixations to flourish. "While not as drawn to porn as men," George Scipione writes, "the Internet replaces the romantic or raunchy novel as a major polluter of women's hearts. I know of several instances of women leaving their husbands and children for a total stranger met online."[37]

While in seminary, my fellow students and I used to joke about another "dangers of the Internet" sermon from the latest guest preacher in chapel. But not long after I became a pastor, I understood why. I have seen firsthand how enslavement to Internet temptations can ruin lives. I have watched men, women, marriages, and ministries destroyed by such fixations. Marital infidelity always involves fixation. When you fixate, other perceptions are blocked. The fixation can completely fill your view, commanding all your attention and even crowding out the full realization that what you are doing is wrong. Don't underestimate the usefulness of the Internet to Satan, or the power your sin nature can gain over you when it feeds on corrupt fixations. The war against sin and temptation is real. Watch what you focus on, or you may begin losing the battle before you even know it has begun.

Pray, Confess, Change

In all that you do, remember that you cannot resist temptation, grow in holiness, or even escape infidelity without God's continual grace and care. After all, you and I are still sinners in a world saturated with temptations, and, absent God's grace, we will do as sinners have always done. In order to guard your heart you must rely on God. You must pray to God. Ask him to keep you from temptation, to minimize the impact of temptation, and to give you the power to reject temptation, whatever that might mean under the circumstances. Memorize the following brief passage of Scripture and let it remind, encourage, and empower you whenever you face sexual temptation.

> Since, then, you have been raised with Christ, set your hearts on things above, where Christ is seated at the right hand of God. Set your minds on things above, not on earthly things. For you died, and your life is now hidden with Christ in God. When Christ, who is your life, appears, then you also will appear with him in glory. Put to death, therefore, whatever belongs to your earthly nature: sexual immorality, impurity, lust, evil desires and greed, which is idolatry.

Colossians 3:1–5

And always remember that while prayer, God's grace, and the power of Scripture are all absolutely necessary, so is obedience, which in this area is quite clear. Don't be where you ought not to be, and don't fixate on anything you shouldn't. In other words, "Above all else, guard your heart, for it is the wellspring of life" (Proverbs 4:23).

Life After Sexual Sin

As with the chapter on choosing a spouse, some of you may have read this chapter and begun to feel a burden of guilt, sin, or pain. Perhaps you have permitted fixation to take hold, whether involving a person or pornography. You know you have been allowing the fire of temptation to spread, maybe so much so that the act of committing adultery in your heart is a familiar occurrence.

Or maybe it's worse. Perhaps you have acted on your temptation, even to the point of actual adultery. Maybe your self-indulgence has all gone much farther than at one time you could have possibly imagined, and you simply don't know what to do.

No one is immune to the danger of sexual sin. Every Christian has committed some form of it, particularly as defined by Jesus. But whatever your situation, no matter how far gone, no matter how shameful or shocking, in Christ there is hope, forgiveness, and mercy. Even David, a man after God's own heart, committed adultery. While David had to pay the earthly costs for his transgression, Psalm 51 reminds us that, after confessing and repenting of his sin, he experienced God's forgiveness. God created a new heart in David and he can do the same for you.

On the other hand, maybe you are the faithful spouse who has suffered awful pain from an adulterous husband or wife. In either case, there is much to be learned from an event recounted in John, chapter 8.

One day, a group of powerful men brought before Jesus a woman who had been caught in adultery (John 8:3–11).[38] Jesus turned to these men and said, "If any one of you is without sin, let him be the first to throw a stone at her." Jesus understood what was in the hearts and minds of men. He understood that we all struggle with sin, and that sexual sin in one's thought life can be a common occurrence. Indeed, not one man was willing to throw a stone, and gradually they began to leave.

If you have been unfaithful in marriage, mentally or physically, see yourself as that adulterous woman. For when all her accusers had gone, something remarkable happened. Jesus turned to her, forgave her, and presented her with this command, "Go now and leave your life of sin" (John 8:11). As you turn to him in repentance, Jesus will freely forgive you, too, and will give you the very same command. "Go now and leave your life of sin."

If it is your spouse who has been unfaithful, see yourself as those who accused the adulterer. Certainly, there is no question that you have suffered and been betrayed. But recognize this also: each of us are capable of any sin if we are put in the right circumstances. Even you. Moreover, each of us have sinful tendencies in particular areas. It can be very hard to understand the power of one person's temptations if you also are not weak in those areas. Yes, your spouse has failed horribly, but this gives you no right to cast a stone or to insist on condemnation. Christ has forgiven you for countless sins against his own holiness, and kept on loving you freely and fully. You likewise have grace from God to forgive your spouse, and to love him or her with the love that comes from your Savior, who suffered on the cross for you, your Christian spouse, and all who would believe.

PART SIX

Children

A Proverbs-Driven Life accepts the calling to raise children as a task delegated and directed by God.

11

Born Foolish

A Child's Need for Discipline

Folly is bound up in the heart of a child, but the rod of discipline will drive it far from him.

Proverbs 22:15

I used to be an expert on raising and disciplining children. I possessed deep, biblical insights into all the rich dynamics and subtle intricacies of parent-child interactions. I saw clearly how God's Word can speak into every situation, illuminating each childrearing moment with perfect clarity and providing the ideal course of action. Then something unprecedented happened, something that put all my neat, tidy theories under severe strain.

For the first time, I became a father.

What a shock it was to find that children don't share my sophisticated perspective on how to raise them! In fact, from a very young age they seem to demonstrate a firm belief in some completely different view. At first, I didn't handle this very well.

169

Today, by God's grace, I am a far better parent than I was when our children were infants. And I know that while there is a great deal of clear guidance in Scripture about raising children, it's not as easy to apply as I once thought! I realize now that one of the key factors I didn't grasp in my first years as a father (much less during my "expert" phase) is that every time a parent interacts with a child, there are two sinners in the room, not just one. That's why both these chapters on childrearing are written from the same premise: Children may be born foolish, helpless, and ignorant, but it is their parents who are the truly needy ones.

What is Biblical Discipline?

Raising children is one of the most challenging, painful, and joyous experiences we can encounter. It is also incredibly and immeasurably significant to the kingdom of God. If you have children, there is no more important calling in your life than to raise them according to the "training and instruction of the Lord" (Ephesians 6:4).

The book of Proverbs demonstrates the importance of parental discipline by the sheer amount of attention it gives to the subject. Indeed, discipline of children is a major focus of Proverbs. But let's be clear that when Proverbs speaks of "discipline" it has in view quite a range of activities. In Proverbs, "discipline" includes *instruction, teaching, training* and *correction*. Stated very briefly, *instruction* and *teaching* involve imparting knowledge; *training* involves all sorts of coaching and preparation; and *correction* involves identifying errors and urging their removal. In other words, biblical discipline is fundamentally about passing along and reinforcing wisdom and truth in a variety of ways; it's about education. In that sense, the entire Book of Proverbs involves discipline of the young! As Daniel Estes writes, "Even a cursory reading of the book of Proverbs reveals that it is dominated by the subject of education.

The voice of the teacher addressing his pupils resounds from its pages."[39] Truly, the book of Proverbs is the most extensive and explicit resource on childrearing in the entire Bible.

How interesting, then, that Proverbs teaches no single method of parental discipline. Nor is there any one proverb or passage that captures everything we need to know in order to raise children well. Instead, Proverbs provides a rich fabric of teaching woven from many individual strands. This means parents must do more than learn a few key verses about child-rearing—we must pursue God's wisdom on the topic.

In the raising of children, God has in mind that everyone involved, parents and children alike, would grow in wisdom. So as we begin our discussion, we want to start by seeking clarity on the purpose of discipline.

Why Discipline?

Motivations always matter to God, and why we choose to take a particular approach to childrearing is certainly no exception. Christians frequently make the mistake of bringing a worldly mindset to the topic of raising kids. In our pragmatic age, we too easily jump over the "why" questions so we can get to work on the "how." Yet the "why" is vitally important and reveals our worldview. You see, God is interested in more than the use of biblical methods. He wants us to employ those methods *out of a biblical motivation*. Thus, in this chapter, we must first examine *why* God wants us to discipline our children. Proverbs reveals three motivations for this: For our children's sake, our neighbors' sake, and our own sake. Of course, we also do it for God's glory.

For Our Children's Sake

> He who spares the rod hates his son, but he who loves him is careful to discipline him.
>
> Proverbs 13:24

The book of Proverbs tells us that the primary motivation for disciplining our children is love. This motivation is most clearly articulated in Proverbs 13:24, above. Bruce Waltke explains the teaching of this proverb:

> Loving parents seek to correct the faults of their children because . . . their children's lives, favor, protection, healing, dignity and prosperity are at stake. Unloving parents turn their backs on them and hand them over to death, social ruin, public exposure, calamity, and shameful poverty.[40]

That can seem like harsh language in a day when popular culture constantly tells us that people are naturally good and therefore, left to themselves, will make good decisions and "do the right thing." But we must recall that the entire point of the Bible is that man is naturally so sinful and wicked that the Son of God had to come and give his life for our sake. We must remind ourselves continually to reject the unbiblical teachings of secular culture. Left entirely to themselves, children *will* follow harmful paths. Unless they are *given* discipline, they will not *gain* discipline.

Undisciplined children, then, tend to grow into undisciplined adults, becoming a danger to themselves (and others). A child who never learned to live within the boundaries of his parents' rules will be more likely as an adult to overstep the boundaries of God's moral law. In the long run, these children pay a high price for their parents' neglect, for society is not kind to the undisciplined adult.

According to Proverbs 19:18 and 23:13–14, poorly trained children can even suffer premature death. Of those young people who die tragically from being involved in drugs or crime, for example, how many do you imagine had careful, attentive, loving, biblical upbringings? Surely it is no exaggeration to say that the more neglectful the parent, the more unloving; and the more loving the parent, the more that they attend to discipline with great care.

Consider Hophni and Phineas, sons of Eli, a priest of Israel. The Israelite priesthood being hereditary, Hophni and Phineas had priestly duties, yet they "were wicked men; they had no regard for the LORD" (1 Samuel 2:12). They treated the offerings of the Lord with contempt and committed sexual sin with women who served at the entrance to the tent of meeting. God expressed his anger and judgment in 1 Samuel 3:13, "For I told [Eli] that I would judge his family forever because of the sin he knew about; his sons made themselves contemptible, and *he failed to restrain them*" (emphasis added). Indeed, Hophni and Phineas were soon killed by Philistines, on the same day the ark was captured.

Parents who love their children will not permit them to pay the high cost of an undisciplined life. Wise and loving parents recognize that childhood is the single most important season for character formation. Charles Bridges, in his commentary on Proverbs, writes, "Our character largely takes form of that mould into which our early years were cast. . . . If the crooked shoots of self-will and disobedience are not cut off, their rapid growth and rapidly growing strength will greatly increase the future difficulty of bending them."[41]

How easy it is to ignore a small child's act of sin and rebellion. How simple to favor a short-term peace over the time and effort necessary to correct and teach. But to build a habit of these compromises is to prefer yourself and your momentary comforts above the entire span of your child's life. Parents who seek to live a Proverbs-driven life must take the long view. Certainly, the time to prune "the crooked shoots of self-will and disobedience" is when our children are young, not when they are adults. Wise parents act on the truth that unchecked childhood disobedience can have life-long consequences. Parents who have a godly, sacrificial love for their children take a long view of childrearing. They recognize that biblical love and biblical discipline go hand in hand.

For Our Neighbors' Sake

Better to meet a bear robbed of her cubs than a fool in his folly.

Proverbs 17:12

When a foolish, undisciplined child grows into a foolish, undisciplined adult, the circle of trouble widens. Such adults often go through life towing havoc behind them, and are incapable of influencing society in the direction of anything except shallowness and corruption. Raise a fool, send him or her out into the world, and you have harmed more than your child. You have incrementally damaged your entire culture.

Therefore, a second motivation for faithfully disciplining our children is to help fulfill the command to love my neighbor as I love myself (Luke 10:27). Consider the son who was never made to fulfill his obligations as a child. This boy grows up, becomes a deadbeat dad, and brings years of pain to his wife and children. Consider the daughter who as a child never learned principles of modesty and the control of her sexual desire, and then matures into an adulterer, bringing destruction to entire families. The failure to discipline children has ripple effects far beyond the home.

On the other hand, what greater service could a parent render to society than to raise children whose character will testify to the truth of the gospel for the rest of their lives? Truly, the sacrifice of *personal* discipline necessary to engage in effective *child* discipline is exactly the kind of laying down of one's life to which our Savior has called us (John 15:13).

The sacrifices you make to serve your children serve the world. Don't foist fools on society. If you love your neighbor, you will make every effort to raise godly children.

For Our Own Sake

Discipline your son, and he will give you peace; he will bring delight to your soul.

Proverbs 29:17

A third motivation for applying biblical discipline is that we might experience the rewards of having well-behaved children. Godly children are a source of great joy to their parents, as affirmed in Proverbs 29:17, above. To see a child increasingly learn to control his or her sinful impulses and to become polite, kind, humble, and respectful is truly a delight to a parent's soul. In addition, having obedient children also allows for a life that is—relatively speaking—more peaceful and orderly than if children are unruly and rebellious. With less time needing to be spent on enforcing discipline in the home, more of a parent's time may be given to serving others.

The reverse is also true: "a child left to himself disgraces his mother" (Proverbs 29:15). Indeed, few things shame a parent more than a child's overt and willful disobedience, especially in public. The life of King David demonstrates the pain that can come to a parent who fails to exercise sufficient discipline toward children. J.C. Ryle writes of this in his book, *The Duties of Parents*:

> See, too, the case of David. Who can read without pain the history of his children, and their sins? Ammon's incest, Absalom's murder and proud rebellion, Adonijah's scheming ambition: truly these were grievous wounds for the man after God's own heart to receive from his own house. But was there no fault on his side? I fear there can be no doubt that there was. I find a clue to it all in the account of Adonijah in 1 Kings 1:6 (AV): 'His father had not displeased him at any time in saying, Why has thou done so?' There was the foundation of all the mischief. David was an overindulgent father, a father who let

175

his children have their own way, and he reaped according as he had sown.[42]

I admire Bob Beasley's summary of what Proverbs teaches on this point:

> The book of Proverbs consistently repeats a warning to parents (Proverbs 13:24; 17:21; 19:18; 22:15; 23:13–16). Something will be broken in your home; either your child's will, or your heart. The stripes from the rod of correction will either land on your child's rear end, or on your own. If it is the latter, then both you and your child will feel the pain.[43]

In other words, inasmuch as God calls us to raise our children for him, then either we will discipline our children for their disobedience, or God will discipline us for ours. A wise parent, according to Proverbs, reaps the rewards of discipline and avoids the pain that comes from parental neglect.

For the Glory and Pleasure of God

> Not to us, O LORD, not to us, but to your name be the glory, because of your love and faithfulness.
>
> Psalms 115:1

Finally, as I have already mentioned, godly children are a walking testimony to the truth of God's power through the gospel of Jesus Christ. In many places, such children and young people are so rare that they are easily noticed. This pleases God, and in directing the world's attention to God's goodness and power, these children bring him much glory.

This general idea appears throughout the New Testament. In the Sermon on the Mount Jesus said, "Let your light shine before men, that they may see your good deeds and praise your Father in heaven" (Matthew 5:16). Paul wrote to the Philippians, "Do everything without complaining or arguing, so that you may become blameless and pure, children of God without fault in a crooked and depraved generation, in which you shine like stars in the universe" (Philippians 2:14–15). And Peter urged his readers to "live such good lives among the pagans that, though they accuse you of doing wrong, they may see your good deeds and glorify God on the day he visits us" (1 Peter 2:12).

When children are well-disciplined, it's a win for everyone. The children benefit by reinforcing good habits and growing in godly behavior. Parents are blessed and their lives are made easier. Society benefits because more mature, responsible individuals are joining its ranks. And above all, God is glorified as the behavior of our children points to Christ's redeeming love.

These are the kind of young men and women God is calling parents to raise. In the next chapter—the final chapter of this book—we will find out how that's done.

12

Still Sinners

A Parent's Need for the Grace of God

For these commands are a lamp, this teaching is a light, and
the corrections of discipline are the way to life,

Proverbs 6:23

---

*I*f you are in a parenting stage of life, or hope to be there one
day, my prayer is that the previous chapter was both inspiring
and sobering. God calls parents to a profound stewardship, one
that ought to fill us with wonder and holy awe. What greater
treasure can we be entrusted with than the formation of an eternal soul? Of course, carrying out such a responsibility—day after
day and year after year—is a huge challenge. But God has not
left us alone. In the all-encompassing power of his grace he has
given parents his Word to teach us and his Spirit to empower us,
that we might raise our children for their good, society's good,
our own good, and most importantly for God's glory.

In Proverbs 6:23, above, we see both the promise of grace
and a reminder of what's at stake in parenting. First, this verse

tells us that the commands and teachings of Proverbs *really do* illuminate for us those things we must remember and focus on as we seek to raise children for God. Second, the changes in behavior that result from true biblical discipline *really do* make possible a unique fullness of life in God.

But the verse also implies a need for action. Discipline must be applied to the child from outside. That discipline must result in godly changes—"corrections"—in both thinking and behavior. Only then can the child get on the right path, or "way." If the discipline is not applied, or if it is of a kind that does not produce corrections in thought, word, and deed, then the child cannot even *get on* the path to life. The alternative is obviously some other path—and not one that the Bible calls life.

Where does that leave us as parents? Here we are, holding the future of one or more human souls in our hands. Left to themselves, these precious children will forever remain fools and fail to get on the path of life. As they try to understand who God is and what it means to live a life of faith, they will be looking first and foremost to us—and for much of their childhood they will be looking very closely. In disciplining our children, our ultimate goal is to reveal God to them, a God of love, mercy, compassion, and perfect holiness. But we are weak vessels and sinful creatures who are prone to anger, discouragement, hypocrisy, pride, and inconsistency. None of us are competent in ourselves to parent well. We are sinners called to serve other sinners in the grace God provides.

God intends for such stark realities to leave us in the best possible place: Desperate for him and having no hope in our own abilities, yet confident that he who called us to these things will be faithful. As this book progresses from the "why" of discipline to the "how," may that be the spirit in which you read this final chapter.

Before we jump into the subject, let's recall that in Proverbs "discipline" means education and training in a broad sense. Also remember that Proverbs does not prescribe one single method of discipline, but an array of methods. Paul Wegner makes this point in commenting on an important Hebrew term.

> [T]he Hebrew word *musar*, commonly translated as 'discipline' in the OT, has a wide range of meanings that suggest various levels of discipline, including on one end of the spectrum 'teaching and instruction' (Proverbs 1:2, 3, 7, 4:14), then progressing to 'exhortation or warning' (Ezekiel 5:15; Job 20:3), and climaxing with 'discipline or chastening' (Proverbs 13:24; 22:15; 23:13).[44]

For purposes of this chapter we will reduce the range a step further, looking at *musar* as involving two broad categories, verbal discipline and corporal discipline.

Speak the Truth in Love: Verbal Discipline

While corporal discipline certainly has its place in raising young children, the overwhelming emphasis in Scripture is on training children by speaking to them. In fact, Proverbs teaches that parents should seek to become so effective at verbal discipline that corporal discipline eventually becomes unnecessary. There are two main verbal disciplinary techniques suggested by Proverbs: To encourage good behavior and to discourage bad behavior.

Encourage Good Behavior

> Wisdom is supreme; therefore get wisdom. Though it cost all you have, get understanding. Esteem her, and she will exalt you; embrace her, and she will honor you.
>
> Proverbs 4: 7–8

Wise parents verbally encourage their children toward good behavior. In Proverbs chapter 4, a father shares with his sons wisdom which was originally shared with him by his father.

Listen, my sons, to a father's instruction . . . When I was a boy in my father's house, still tender, and an only child of my mother, he taught me and said . . . Wisdom is supreme; therefore get wisdom. Though it cost all you have, get understanding. Esteem her, and she will exalt you; embrace her, and she will honor you. She will set a garland of grace on your head and present you with a crown of splendor.

Proverbs 4:1, 3, 7–9

Do you see what the words of the grandfather—as recalled by the father who wrote the Proverb—are accomplishing here? They are encouraging the son to prize wisdom by giving him incentives. The father tells his son that if he pursues and respects wisdom he will be both exalted and honored. Indeed, a primary method of discipline throughout Scripture is precisely this sort of verbal encouragement: explaining to our children the benefits of pursuing what is good.

For these verbal incentives to succeed they must be expressed in language the particular child can understand, and this is exactly what the father does here. Apparently this son was old enough to have some interest in the opposite sex, so the father wisely compares the benefits of pursuing and acquiring wisdom with the benefits of finding a wife. The father calls on the son to embrace wisdom as he would a beautiful and godly wife, urging him to see that this will bring him honor in the community. The message is clear: good behavior leads to social success. The father disciplines his son—that is, he helps him *become* more disciplined—by enumerating the advantages that flow from good behavior.

Of course, the analogy of a spouse wouldn't work for a three-year old, but something like this might: "If you do what mommy and daddy tell you to do you will have a very happy life, you will be able to have fun and play in the park." This kind of verbal discipline must be specific to the child and the situation. Effective incentives are those that are tailored to the interests and desires of our own children.

Some people think it's wrong to use incentives in childrearing, that it amounts to bribery. But to tell a child that obedience to parents will lead to a good life is not to set up some kind of transaction. The benefits that flow from obedience are not something we receive *in exchange for* obedience. Rather, God has so arranged this world that wisdom and self-discipline simply lead to a better life than do foolishness and laziness. While God's sovereign care for us is ultimately what makes all this happen, it does not follow that God owes us something when we obey him. If we receive what might be called a reward for such behavior, it is not because we have gained leverage over God, but because he delights to encourage us to even more good behavior.

Throughout Proverbs, and indeed the entire Bible, we are constantly told that God's ways are better *for us*. From God's urging Adam and Eve to stay away from the fruit on the Tree of Life, to the thrilling descriptions of the worship around God's throne described in the Book of Revelation, Scripture is packed with encouragement to live in obedience to God, and benefit as a result.

The apostle Paul comments on the built-in incentive of the fifth commandment as he instructs the children of the church in Ephesus, "Children, obey your parents in the Lord, for this is right. 'Honor your father and mother'— which is the first commandment with a promise—'that it may go well with you and that you may enjoy long life on the earth'" (Ephesians 6:1–3). Jay Adams, reflecting on these words from Paul, writes, "Christians, of all people, should have been the first to recognize and utilize rewards and incentives in teaching discipline to children."[45]

Be lavish with your encouragement toward your children. Reinforce constantly for them the good news of how God's world works. Teach them that obedience and wisdom are the path of life.

Discourage Bad Behavior

My son, if sinners entice you, do not give in to them.

Proverbs 1:10

Life would be a lot simpler for all of us if the other path, the one that is not the path of life, weren't sometimes so appealing. But it is appealing, and the more foolish children are, the more likely they will be to yield to that appeal. That's why, as parents, we must also help our children learn to resist temptation. In addition to verbally encouraging our children to engage in good behavior, Proverbs also tells parents to verbally discourage bad behavior. Not surprisingly, this is done by explaining to them the consequences of disobedience. Proverbs 1 provides a classic example of such an admonition, and verses 10–15 set the stage.

> My son, if sinners entice you, do not give in to them. If they say, 'Come along with us; let's lie in wait for someone's blood, let's waylay some harmless soul; let's swallow them alive, like the grave, and whole, like those who go down to the pit; we will get all sorts of valuable things and fill our houses with plunder; throw in your lot with us, and we will share a common purse'—my son, do not go along with them, do not set foot on their paths.
>
> Proverbs 1:10–15

The first thing the father does in this proverb is warn his son against the corrupting power of social pressure to join a group intent on sin. For at least the last one-hundred years in the West, probably every generation of Christian parents has believed that the secular culture faced by their children is more corrupt than the one the parents faced when they were growing up. And on that point probably every generation of parents has been right. Today, children interact with a uniquely wicked culture in ways that were unimaginable to most people even twenty years ago. The basic call of sin, however, never changes: "Come along with us . . . we will get . . . throw in your lot with us...we will share." This message of companionship, of belonging, joined with an appeal to some sort of gain, is incredibly powerful, especially to youth.

As seen in Proverbs 1, verbal discouragement of bad behavior thus involves both warning and explanation, exposing the sin for what it is. It is vitally important for modern parents to follow the pattern of the father in this proverb by saying to their children essentially what he said to his son, "Do not go along with them, do not set foot on their paths."

But then we must go further, clarifying the consequences of giving in to evil enticements. For in verses 16–19 of Proverbs 1, the father points out that sin never ends well: "These men lie in wait for their own blood; they waylay only themselves! Such is the end of all who go after ill-gotten gain; it takes away the lives of those who get it." Truly, those who plot wickedness fall into their own traps.

Of course, children don't always need to be tempted into making bad decisions—they can do it all by themselves! So whether peer pressure or other cultural influences are directly involved or not, parents must verbally discourage in children any form of foolish or sinful behavior by emphasizing the disincentives. A boy of seven playing with matches should be told not to do so, but he must also be shown the destruction that can result. A girl of thirteen flirting with pre-marital sex should be told to stop, but she should also be informed about the painful consequences of sexually transmitted diseases, the burdens of a teenage pregnancy, and the benefits of abstinence prior to marriage that would be forfeited. Proverbs informs us that wise parents discourage bad behavior in their children by helping them understand the consequences of disobedience.

Speak Purposefully

Better is open rebuke than hidden love.

Proverbs 27:5

More than two dozen times in Proverbs, the reader is urged to "listen" so that he or she might benefit from wisdom. But our children cannot benefit from the wisdom God equips us to bring them if we do not speak. Therefore our speaking must be intentional and purposeful. It must be regular and frequent. And it must be biblical.

The words of discipline we speak to our children need to be clear, true, and loving. Those words that encourage godly behavior must be full of the joy and promise of God's blessing. Those words that discourage sinful behavior must seek to warn and persuade in no uncertain terms, for there is much at stake.

Sometimes parents come to believe that failure to correct their children verbally is itself an act of love. They reason that by keeping silent they are allowing their children "space" to "find their own way." Certainly, as children mature they must be given greater autonomy by degrees. But at any age and any level of maturity sin is sin, foolishness is foolishness, and wisdom is wisdom. Refusal to warn someone of the perils of sin is never an act of love. If in the local church all Christians are called to "Let the word of Christ dwell in you richly as you teach and admonish one another with all wisdom" (Colossians 3:16), then surely this applies in the family as well. (See also Romans 15:14, 1 Thessalonians 5:11, and Hebrews 10:24.)

A central component of any parent's calling in God is therefore to play the role of one who verbally encourages and praises the good, and discourages and rebukes the bad, that children may not be deceived by the constant barrages of secular culture or by their own hearts. Do not allow anything to convince *you* that it is better to stop speaking to your children of sin and holiness. Proverbs rejects this reasoning through the reminder of Proverbs 27:5, above. As a parent you have no right to remain silent. If you love your children you will speak to them, you will rebuke them in love, you will discipline them verbally. Recall, however, what James tells us about our words.

Likewise the tongue is a small part of the body, but it makes great boasts. Consider what a great forest is set on fire by a small spark. The tongue also is a fire, a world of evil among the parts of the body. It corrupts the whole person, sets the whole course of his life on fire, and is itself set on fire by hell.

James 3:5–6

Thus, the primary method by which we are called to warn our children away from their foolishness is perhaps our own greatest point of weakness. This is an irony that should drive us to our knees to seek God for grace.

The Exception, Not the Rule: Corporal Discipline

The second biblical method at a parent's disposal is corporal discipline. Normally discipline should begin with verbal correction, and often that is enough. But especially when children are younger, most parents will find it necessary, on occasion, to couple verbal discipline with corporal discipline.

There are two extremely important differences between verbal discipline and corporal discipline. First, verbal discipline can be appropriate and helpful both before and after a child sins or behaves foolishly. Corporal discipline, on the other hand, is never appropriate except *in response to* a specific instance of sin or foolishness. Second, every instance of corporal discipline must be joined with verbal discipline so that the child understands as clearly as possible why the corporal discipline is being applied. Parents must use words to help their children connect the dots between the sin they committed and the discipline they are receiving. Parents must also use words to convey to their children that they love them. Make sure you hug them too especially when the corporal discipline is over.

Thus, parents who maintain a biblical balance in their approach to child discipline will correct their children verbally far, far more often than they correct them physically—but they *will* correct them physically when necessary. Every parent of younger children who seeks to faithfully apply the biblical teaching on parenting will, at one point or another, need to apply corporal discipline, usually in the form of spanking.

In some quarters, however, any form of corporal discipline is considered highly suspect, if not outright abusive. Certainly, both verbal discipline and corporal discipline can become abusive if used wrongly. However, as noted by biblical scholar Andreas Kostenberger, "Appealing to excessive cases that involve abuse does not justify abandoning spanking as a form of discipline. Children need to learn the consequences of wrong behavior, and spanking can be a useful means to convey that lesson."[46]

Proverbs makes clear that corporal discipline of our children, biblically administered and coupled with verbal discipline, is truly an act of love. Let's look more closely at the Bible's teaching on this topic.

Only for the Obstinate

Wisdom is found on the lips of the discerning, but a rod is for the back of him who lacks judgment.

Proverbs 10:13

By its overwhelming emphasis on the use of words as a training tool, Proverbs teaches that verbal discipline is always to be preferred over corporal discipline. However, when children repeatedly reject the wise counsel of their parents it reflects more than a simple lack of discernment. It reveals that they are rebellious and obstinate; they are fools, lacking judgment.

According to Proverbs, persistent foolishness must eventually be met with a corporal response. As seen in Proverbs 10:13, above, corporal discipline of children is reserved for those who obstinately refuse to listen to godly instruction. The language used in Proverbs regarding fools is not polite. It certainly wouldn't pass any tests of political correctness, and its characterization of obstinate children may not be pleasing to parents who find it difficult to see beyond the charms of their young ones. Consider the imagery of Proverbs 26:3, for example: "A whip for the horse, a halter for the donkey, and a rod for the backs of fools!" Here, those who obstinately reject verbal correction are compared to stubborn animals to whom language means little or nothing.

The application to parenting is that when words fail, children still must be trained—and by that point all that is left is corporal discipline. Children who will not receive verbal correction must receive a different, more direct, form of correction.

The Promise of Effectiveness

The rod of correction imparts wisdom.

Proverbs 29:15

Proverbs teaches more than the *necessity* of corporal discipline for the obstinate child. It teaches the *effectiveness* of corporal discipline. When Proverbs 22:15 says, "Folly is bound up in the heart of a child, but the rod of discipline will drive it far from him," we see that the rod can make a real difference. Commenting on Proverbs 29:15, above, Pastor Tedd Tripp writes, "The rod of correction brings wisdom to the child. It provides an immediate tactile demonstration of the foolishness of rebellion."[47]

This is never the easy path for parents; ignoring a child's sin and pretending all will be well is far more convenient. But when a young child will not respond to verbal discipline, the "immediate tactile demonstration" of the rod is an act of sacrificial parental love that will help the child grow in wisdom.

Of Techniques and Motivations

Fathers, do not exasperate your children; instead, bring them up in the training and instruction of the Lord.

Ephesians 6:4

As I began this section on corporal discipline, I noted two techniques important to a parent's use of it. While corporal discipline is ultimately intended to *prevent future sin*, it is only to be used *in response to past sin*. Also, corporal discipline and verbal discipline must go hand in hand, so that the child knows you love him or her, and knows *why* he or she is being corrected in this way.

Here is a third very important point of technique—the corporal discipline "must fit the crime." Parents must be certain they are not engaging in what Jay Adams refers to as "over-discipline." Adams defines this as using "sledge hammers to drive thumb tacks."[48] The term may also be applied to overly frequent and undiscerning use of corporal discipline. The irony is that these errors actually reduce the effectiveness of corporal discipline. Charles Bridges wisely admonishes parents to recognize that the rod "is medicine, not food; the remedy for occasional diseases of the constitution, not the daily regimen for life and nourishment. To convert medicine into daily food gradually destroys its remedial quality."[49] A wise parent knows when to use corporal discipline, and when not to.

When considering corporal discipline, parents must also pay close attention to their own motivations; they must examine their hearts. First, parents must never discipline their children out of frustration or anger. Corporal discipline should always be motivated by love for the child and exercised in a spirit of self-control. This is central to redemptive, biblical corporal correction. A wise parent always remembers that love, not

189

angry self-righteousness, is the only appropriate motivation and the only biblical motivation for corporal discipline. Proverbs never associates parental discipline with anger, but with love. Consider, for example, Proverbs 13:24, "He who spares the rod *hates* his son, but he who *loves* him is careful to discipline him" (emphasis added).

Closely related to the error of anger and self-righteousness is the error of a parent who exercises corporal discipline to try to preserve his or her own authority. This ought never to be the reason we move from verbal discipline to corporal discipline. To discipline for the sake of our own authority makes the discipline primarily about ourselves, when it is supposed to be about God and our children. The only biblical reason to administer corporal discipline is because we want to save our children from the consequences of disobedience. Tedd Tripp provides this helpful reminder regarding the ultimate purpose of corporal discipline, "The issue is not a parental insistence on being obeyed. The issue is the child's need to be rescued from death—the death that results from rebellion left unchallenged in the heart."[50]

Finally, angry and self-righteous parents bring a spirit of punishment into their corporal discipline that is completely out of place, unbiblical, inappropriate, and counterproductive. Corporal discipline of children is never characterized in Proverbs as a matter of retribution or pure punishment. In the Bible translation used for this book, the English word "punish" does appear twice (and only twice) referring to children, in Proverbs 23:13–14. However, other versions translate the Hebrew more accurately, putting the emphasis on the *physical act* of striking, not the *motivation behind* the act.

God does not punish believers for their sin, because all our punishment was borne by Christ on the cross. Rather, as we will see in the following section, God comes to us in mercy, not vengefulness. He does not punish us in anger or retribution. He disciplines us in mercy that we might learn and grow. Thus, as we model God to our children, our discipline must be similarly motivated by a merciful desire to love and serve, not a vengeful desire to punish. In corporal discipline there must never be any hint of retribution or payback. Our goal in corporal discipline is not to force a child to pay a price, but to help him or her understand the seriousness of sin and the importance of gaining wisdom.

God's Discipline

There is no doubt about it, disciplining children is hard work. It is a marathon, not a sprint. It requires energy, persistence, and unshakeable commitment. Often it does not yield immediate rewards. However, as we have seen in these two chapters, there are many excellent reasons for disciplining our children in a spirit of patience and endurance.

Such parenting demonstrates love for our neighbor as we raise children who will be better employees, citizens, spouses, and parents. Such parenting demonstrates our love for our children, saves them from destruction, and brings us delight and joy. Such parenting demonstrates a love for God's glory and exaltation, because godly children underscore the truth of Scripture and display the redemptive power of the gospel. These are all wonderful reasons for parents to be encouraged as they seek to discipline their children faithfully. However, there is one more encouragement that is helpful to discuss and understand separately. The Bible reveals that in disciplining our children biblically we imitate our loving, heavenly Father who so faithfully disciplines his children—us.

God Disciplines Us Verbally

Hear, O my people, and I will warn you—if you would but listen to me, O Israel!

Psalm 81:8

191

When parents verbally instruct, encourage, and rebuke their children they are imitating God who does the same for us. The primary way God speaks to us is through his written Word. The Bible is nothing less than God's impartation to us of everything we need to know on this earth about him, his ways, his purposes, his Son, and how we ought to live in relationship to him and to one another. In it we find laws, statutes, commandments, wisdom, and more. Through his Word, God both rebukes us and encourages us. In the Bible, God sets before us the consequences of bad behavior and the benefits of good behavior, and calls us to follow the path of righteousness. God's Word trains us.

The Bible also reveals that God's verbal disciplining of his children is motivated by love and mercy. Consider, for example, the first few chapters of Revelation, in which Jesus verbally admonishes, instructs, and encourages his church. Why does he do this? The answer comes in Revelation 3:19, "Those whom I love I rebuke and discipline. So be earnest, and repent." Like the father in Proverbs who wants only good for his children, God says to us, "Listen, my son."

God Disciplines Us Corporally

My son, do not despise the LORD's discipline and do not resent his rebuke, because the LORD disciplines those he loves, as a father the son he delights in.

Proverbs 3:11–12

Also, when parents corporally correct their children in love, they likewise imitate God. For example, in the twelfth chapter of the epistle to the Hebrews, the author quotes from Proverbs 3:11–12, above, applying it to a congregation undergoing persecution for the sake of Christ. In essence, the writer to the Hebrews tells them God is using their pain and suffering to corporally discipline them—to help them mature and grow. (These sufferings appear to have included imprisonment, loss of property, and expulsion from the synagogue and temple.) Note how the writer connects the concept of the discipline of an earthly father to the discipline of our heavenly Father:

> Moreover, we have all had human fathers who disciplined us and we respected them for it. How much more should we submit to the Father of our spirits and live! Our fathers disciplined us for a little while as they thought best; but God disciplines us for our good, that we may share in his holiness.
>
> Hebrews 12:9–10

We also see that the fact that God is corporally disciplining these Hebrew Christians is proof that he is their Father and they are his legitimate offspring. "It is for discipline that you endure; God deals with you as with sons; for what son is there whom his father does not discipline? But if you are without discipline, of which all have become partakers, then you are illegitimate children and not sons" (Hebrews 12:7–8).

Finally, the writer notes that while it's no fun to be on the receiving end of corporal discipline, it does bring great rewards. "No discipline seems pleasant at the time, but painful. Later on, however, it produces a harvest of righteousness and peace for those who have been trained by it" (Hebrews 12:11).

As with the rest of Scripture, these verses, written to a group of God's people who lived long ago, hold timeless truth for us today. These words are written to us. They remind us that God continues to discipline us corporally. He does this because we are his children, and therefore he loves us like a father, extends mercy to us, and desires what is best for us—even when what is best is not what is most pleasant.

So we see that in the final analysis, biblical discipline is about parents leaning on God for grace as they seek to discipline their children in the same ways that God disciplines us. When discipline is done well (and no parents do it perfectly—that's why we need grace!) we reveal to our children something of the nature of God, and thereby position them for a life of serving him.

Epilogue
The End of Wisdom

*H*ave you ever watched one of those experiments where a mouse in a maze is trying to find his way to the cheese? The mouse frequently heads in the wrong direction, hits a wall, and has to turn back to try another path. Eventually, he makes it through and enjoys his reward.

As I get older, I feel a growing kinship with that mouse. My life has often felt like a maze filled with perplexing obstacles. Like the mouse, I've often been confronted with options which, at first glance, seem equally appealing and equally destined for success, only to later find that my choice has led me to a dead end. Like the mouse, I've spent a good deal of time having to backtrack and restart my journey. As a pastor, I witnessed many other people similarly struggling through their own life mazes.

In all this, I've noticed something. Everyone who is working his or her way through the maze of life would like some help knowing which way to go. We're all looking for a guidance system to help us make better choices about matters such as work, marriage, friendships and associations, money and wealth, the use of words, and child rearing. As we've seen in this book, God has given us a guidance system for these matters in the book of Proverbs.

But as we've also seen throughout this book, we must not confuse wisdom with a set of formulas for guaranteed results. Sometimes our desire for answers leads us to demand things of the book of Proverbs it was not intended to deliver. Many people have wished they could treat Proverbs like one of those novelty Magic 8 Balls, seeking unequivocal answers to any possible question. But Proverbs is not like that. Wisdom is not like that. Wisdom requires work. It requires us to think. As I noted in chapter 1, Graeme Goldsworthy tells us that in Proverbs, "God gives the framework for godly thinking but he will not do our thinking for us. We are responsible for the decisions we make as we seek to be wise (to think in a godly way) and to avoid being foolish (to think in a godless way)."[51]

This book represents an initial effort to help you to recognize and take advantage of the framework for godly thinking that Proverbs provides. But I can only take you so far. This is not a self-help book, and I can't guarantee success in thirty days or your money back. I can't even guarantee success in thirty years! Like that mouse in the maze, you and I will continue to take some wrong turns and hit some dead ends. But I can make one guarantee to you—if you look to God for wisdom, he will give it you. I can make that guarantee because God makes it to all of us in the epistle of James, "If any of you lacks wisdom, he should ask God, who gives generously to all without finding fault, and it will be given to him" (James 1:5).

I can also make one other guarantee to you. If you look to God for wisdom, and search for it as for hidden treasure, you will ultimately navigate the maze of life successfully. You will come to know the end, the purpose, of wisdom. Certainly, the *beginning* of wisdom is the fear of the Lord (Proverbs 1:7), but what is the *end* of wisdom? It is the privilege of knowing

God. You see, the reward at the end of our maze is the glorious privilege of knowing Christ and the power of his resurrection. The end of wisdom is God himself.

So as you continue on the journey through the maze that is your life, remember that you are not alone. Your Father is with you. He is counseling you with his wisdom. He's providing light to your path. He stands ready to forgive you for your foolishness and sin. He is leading you inexorably to himself. That is the true end of wisdom. That is the end of the Proverbs-driven life.

Notes

1. Bruce K. Waltke, *The Book of Proverbs Chapters 1–15: NICOT* (Grand Rapids, MI: Eerdmans, 2004), 109.

2. Raymond Dillard and Tremper Longman, *An Introduction to the Old Testament* (Grand Rapids, MI: Zondervan, 1994), 245.

3. Graeme Goldsworthy, *According to Plan: The Unfolding Revelation of God in the Bible* (Downers Grove, IL: Inter-Varsity Press, 1991), 176.

4. Bob Beasley, *The Wisdom of Proverbs* (San Diego, CA: Legacy Press, 2002), ix.

5. Tremper Longman, *Proverbs: Baker Commentary on the Old Testament Wisdom and Psalms* (Grand Rapids, MI: Baker Academic, 2006), 356.

6. James Patterson and Peter Kim, *The Day America Told the Truth* (New York: Prentice Hall Press, 1991).

7. Cited in the article "The Rise of Workplace Slackers" by Al Lewis of *The Denver Post*. A summary of this article appeared in the periodical *The Week* on June 23, 2006, page 46.

8. Cited in the article "The Rise of Workplace Slackers" by Al Lewis of *The Denver Post*. A summary of this article appeared in the periodical *The Week* on June 23, 2006, page 46.

9. Paul Helm, *The Callings: The Gospel in the World* (Carlisle, PA: Banner of Truth, 1987), x.

10. Charles Bridges, *Proverbs* (Carlisle, PA: Banner of Truth, reprinted 1998), 61.

11. While this text addresses slaves, most commentators believe it is appropriate to apply this text to our modern employer-employee relationship.

12. Bruce K. Waltke, *The Book of Proverbs Chapters 1–15: NICOT* (Grand Rapids, MI: Eerdmans, 2004), 339.

13. Charles Bridges, *Proverbs* (Carlisle, PA: Banner of Truth, reprinted 1998), 493.

14. "I am indebted here to the insights of Bruce K. Waltke. See Bruce K. Waltke, *The Book of Proverbs Chapters 1–15: NICOT* (Grand Rapids, MI: Eerdmans, 2004), 482–483 and *The Book of Proverbs Chapters 15–31: NITCOT*, (Grand Rapids, MI: Eerdmans, 2005), 153–154."

15. Gordon Marino, "The Latest Industry to Founder: Ethics Inc.," *The Wall Street Journal*, July 30, 2002. http://online.wsj.com/article/0,,SB1027991654743763960.djm,00.html

16. Bruce K. Waltke, *The Book of Proverbs Chapters 16–31: NICOT* (Grand Rapids, MI: Eerdmans, 2004), 25.

17. "New Study Shows Trends in Tithing and Donating," April 18, 2008, www.barna.org.

18. For example, the Barna Study notes, "During the first five years of the decade, an average of 84 cents out of every dollar donated by born again adults went to churches. In the past three years, though, the proportion has declined to just 76 cents out of every donated dollar."

19. Source: http://truthaboutcredit.org.

20. Charles Bridges, *Proverbs* (Carlisle, PA: Banner of Truth, reprinted 1998), 166–167.

21. J.R.R. Tolkien, *The Fellowship of the Ring* (Boston, MA: Houghton Mifflin, 1994), 85.

22. "Cited by Lewis in a letter to MacMillian publishing company. As quoted in Alan Jacobs', *The Narnian: The Life and Imagination of C.S. Lewis* (NY, NY: Harper Collins, 2005), xix.

23. Charles Bridges, *Proverbs* (Carlisle, PA: Banner of Truth, reprinted 1998), 504.

24. William Arnot, *Studies in Proverbs* (Grand Rapids, MI: Kregel, 1978), 380.

25. Iain Duguid, *Living in the Gap Between Promise and Reality: The Gospel According to Abraham* (Phillipsburg, NJ: P & R Publishing, 1999), 35.

26. Paul E. Koptak, *Proverbs: The NIV Application Commentary* (Grand Rapids, MI: Zondervan, 2003), 470.

27. William Arnot, *Studies in Proverbs* (Grand Rapids, MI: Kregel, 1978), 241.

28. Ibid.

29. From an article in *The Detroit News* as quoted in Edward K. Rowell's, *1001 Quotes, Illustrations & Humorous Stories* (Grand Rapids, MI: Baker Books, 1996), 541.

30. James Patterson and Peter Kim, *The Day America Told the Truth* (New York: Prentice Hall Press, 1991).

31. Ibid.

32. Charles Bridges, *Proverbs* (Carlisle, PA: Banner of Truth, reprinted 1998), 58.

33. Ibid.

34. George Scipione, "Is Porn Norm? From the Back Street to the Main Street," *Evangelium*, vol. 3, issue 4, Sept/Oct 2005, page 2.

35. Philip Graham Ryken, *Written in Stone* (Wheaton, IL: Crossway, 2003), 158.

36. Ibid., 163.

37. George Scipione, "Is Porn Norm? From the Back Street to the Main Street," *Evangelium*, vol. 3, issue 4, Sept/Oct 2005, page 5, footnote 2.

38. Some scholars believe this account was not originally part of John's Gospel. However, even many of these scholars concede that this account was likely a real event which took place in the life and ministry of Jesus.

39. Daniel J. Estes, *Hear, My Son: Teaching and Learning in Proverbs 1–9*. New Studies in Biblical Theology, ed. D.A. Carson (Downers Grove, IL: IVP, 1997), 13.

40. Bruce K. Waltke, *The Book of Proverbs Chapters 1–15: NICOT* (Grand Rapids, MI: Eerdmans, 2004), 574.

41. Charles Bridges, *Proverbs* (Carlisle, PA: Banner of Truth, reprinted 1998), 403.

42. As quoted in Bruce Ray's, *Withhold Not Correction* (Philipsburg, NJ: P & R, 1975), 37–38.

43. Bob Beasley, *The Wisdom of Proverbs* (San Diego, CA: Legacy Press, 2002), 546.

44. Paul D. Wegner, "To Spank or Not to Spank?" *Journal of the Evangelical Theological Society*, vol. 48, no. 4, December 2005, pgs. 719–720.

45. Jay Adams, *Christian Living in the Home* (Philipsburg, NJ: P & R, 1972), 118.

46. Andreas Kostenberger, *God, Marriage, and Family* (Wheaton, IL: Crossway, 2004), 159.

47. Tedd Tripp, *Shepherding a Child's Heart* (Wapwallopen, PA: Shepherd Press, 1995), 107.

48. Jay Adams, *Christian Living in the Home* (Philipsburg, NJ: P & R, 1972), 114–115.

49. As quoted by Bruce Ray in *Withhold Not Correction* (Philipsburg, NJ: P & R, 1978), 95.

50. Tedd Tripp, *Shepherding a Child's Heart* (Wapwallopen, PA: Shepherd Press, 1995), 107.

51. Graeme Goldsworthy, *According to Plan: The Unfolding Revelation of God in the Bible* (Downers Grove, IL: Inter-Varsity Press, 1991), 176.

Anthony T. Selvaggio is presently serving as Theologian in Residence in the Rochester Reformed Presbyterian Church (RPCNA), Rochester, NY. He previously served as the Senior Pastor of the College Hill Reformed Presbyterian Church (RPCNA) in Beaver Falls, PA. He is also a visiting professor at the Reformed Presbyterian Theological Seminary in Pittsburgh, PA. He is an active preacher and frequent conference speaker. He received his Juris Doctor (J.D.) from the University at Buffalo School of Law and his Masters of Divinity from the Reformed Presbyterian Theological Seminary. His published work includes *The Prophets Speak of Him: Encountering Jesus in the Minor Prophets*, (Evangelical Press, 2006), *What the Bible Teaches About Marriage* (Evangelical Press, 2007), *A Proverbs Driven Life* (Shepherd Press, 2008) and *24/7 Christian: Expository Thoughts on James* (Evangelical Press, 2008). He also edited and contributed to *The Faith Once Delivered* (P & R Publishing, 2007). He lives in Rochester, New York with his wife, Michelle, and his two children, Katherine and James. He is also employed in the wealth management field.